We have long known that storytelling is
transmit information between human b
to Sales uses this proven, but underut.
strate how quality tools and techniques can be used to make significant
improvements during the initial interaction between any organization and
its customers.
> —Jack West
> Westinghouse Electric Corporation

. . . couldn't put it down until I had finished it. . . . It is a really good read,
well worth your time!
> —from the Foreword by Thomas J. Murrin
> Dean, Palumbo School of Business Administration,
> Duquesne University and Former Deputy Secretary,
> U.S. Department of Commerce

I'll be putting this one on top of the recommended reading list for my clients.
> —George A. Palmer
> Sales and Marketing Consultant

The book is great! The case studies examined give one the faith that TQM
can be done and done meaningfully. . . . I will be referring to [the book] in
designing our approach to injecting TQM into our marketing/sales effort.
> —Timothy B. Hays
> Director of Marketing
> Metsch Refractories, Inc.

This isn't hard-to-use or impossible-to-fathom theory; it's ready to use
actions, packaged in a series of narratives that are downright fun to read.
Enjoy and learn at the same time!
> —Jeffrey Neubauer
> Marketing Manager
> PPG Industries, Inc.

. . . Applying Total Quality to Sales is an absolute must read and
reread for anyone remotely connected with sales or customer service. It's
truly the sales bible.
> —Peter J. Waterkotte
> Senior Vice President
> Dudreck, DePaul, Ficco, & Morgan, Inc.

Among the many concepts put forth and demonstrated by Welch and Geissler is this, the most fundamental and important of all: successful companies and managers allow nothing to interfere with the close and supportive relationships with customers that customers expect and deserve. I urge anyone concerned with sales to read this book. There's at least one helpful idea on every page.

> —Tom Moore
> Director of Sales and Marketing
> Industrial Appraisal Company

It is my personal conviction that the principles of total quality are applicable to all functions and disciplines in an organization. [This book] demonstrates that fact convincingly with excellent practical examples of actions and results.

> —J. Robert Graham
> Vice President, Corporate Quality Process
> Medrad Technology for People

APPLYING
TOTAL QUALITY
TO SALES

Also available from Quality Press

Bringing Total Quality to Sales
Cas Welch and Pete Geissler

Selling with Excellence: A Quality Approach for Sales Professionals
Larry McCloskey

The Service/Quality Solution: Using Service Management to Gain Competitive Advantage
David A. Collier

The Quality Toolbox
Nancy R. Tague

The ASQC Total Quality Management Series

TQM: *Leadership for the Quality Transformation*
Richard S. Johnson

TQM: *Management Processes for Quality Operations*
Richard S. Johnson

TQM: *The Mechanics of Quality Processes*
Richard S. Johnson and Lawrence E. Kazense

TQM: *Quality Training Practices*
Richard S. Johnson

To request a complimentary catalog of publications, call 800-248-1946

APPLYING TOTAL QUALITY TO SALES

CAS WELCH AND PETE GEISSLER

ASQC Quality Press
Milwaukee, Wisconsin

APPLYING TOTAL QUALITY TO SALES
Cas Welch and Pete Geissler

Library of Congress Cataloging-in-Publication Data

Welch, Cas, 1932–
    Applying total quality to sales / Cas Welch and Pete Geissler.
      p. cm.
    ISBN 0-87389-283-6
    1. Marketing—Management—Case studies. 2. Sales management—Case
studies. 3. Total quality management—Case studies. I. Geissler,
Pete, 1933– . II. Title.
HF5415.13.W418 1995
658.8'1—dc20

94-23665
CIP

10 9 8 7 6 5 4 3 2 1

ISBN 0-87389-283-6

Acquisitions Editor: Susan Westergard
Project Editor: Jeanne W. Bohn
Production Editor: Annette Wall
Marketing Administrator: Mark Olson
Set in Novarese by Linda J. Shepherd.
Cover design by Artistic License.
Printed and bound by BookCrafters, Inc.

ASQC Mission: To facilitate continuous improvement and increase customer satisfaction by identifying, communicating, and promoting the use of quality principles, concepts, and technologies; and thereby be recognized throughout the world as the leading authority on, and champion for, quality.

For a free copy of the ASQC Quality Press Publications Catalog, including ASQC membership information, call 800-248-1946.

Printed in the United States of America

  Printed on acid-free recycled paper

 ASQC
Quality Press
611 East Wisconsin Avenue
Milwaukee, Wisconsin 53202

Dedicated to our children: Meaghan, Mark, Michael,
Maureen, and Molly Welch; and Karl, Bill, Jeff,
and Linde Geissler. Each in his or her unique way taught
us the deepest and most profound meanings of
quality, value, and happiness.

CONTENTS

FOREWORD

Before deciding to write this foreword to *Applying Total Quality to Sales*, I requested a draft copy of the book. Soon thereafter, on a plane ride from Phoenix to Pittsburgh, I took the draft out of my briefcase—and couldn't put it down until I had finished it. Though I've been a *nut* on total quality management for many years—in industry, government, and now in academe—I found Cas and Pete's latest book to be very informative and stimulating, and written in a captivating style.

The book draws heavily on five varied real-world total quality management applications, contributing greatly to the credibility of the authors' suggestions and insights.

Also, it demonstrates how total quality management can and should be applied to functions other than manufacturing. This should serve to motivate many readers to do the same, especially to apply total quality management to the sales function, which so often directly and crucially involves an organization's key customers.

It is a really good read, well worth your time!

Thomas J. Murrin
Dean, A.J. Palumbo School of
Business Administration, Duquesne University;
former deputy secretary, U.S. Department
of Commerce, where he helped initiate
the Malcolm Baldrige National Quality Award;
and former president,
Energy and Advanced Technology Group,
Westinghouse Electric Corporation,
where he elevated productivity and
quality improvement to a key corporate function.

PREFACE

Applying Total Quality to Sales is written for every person in business concerned with and motivated toward improving the effectiveness of the sales, marketing, and quality functions: salespersons, sales managers, marketing and total quality managers, CEOs, and others. All can benefit from the experiences of the five companies profiled here, experiences narrated firsthand by the people who lived them, experiences that can steer readers toward techniques that have worked and away from techniques that have been less productive.

Applying is the operative word in the title. This book is about applying principles and techniques to specific sales processes, and how the application changes the processes and businesses to be more productive and profitable. *Applying* distills the abstract imperatives and principles of total quality management and brings them to the realities of day-to-day operations, the countless details of the sales process, which, when managed creatively, move an order from entry to fulfillment most smoothly, quickly, and profitably.

The authors wish to thank all of the busy executives who contributed to the case studies: Rob Cochran and Cecilia Hoelsher of #1 Cochran, Chester Howell and Ken Boston of Xerox, Jeff Boetticher and Paul Leger of Black Box, Paul and Betty Connelly of Construction Tool Services, and Walter Bridges and Barbara Riggs of Moore Business Forms. All patiently explained their experiences, then reviewed and corrected drafts, and, finally, agreed that the manuscript met the highest standards of quality and was worthy of publication.

CHAPTER 1

LOOKING BACK TO SEE THE FUTURE

Readers' responses to our first book, *Bringing Total Quality to Sales* (Welch and Geissler, 1992), prompted this sequel, a clear demonstration that we, the authors, practice as well as report the successes of having "a sharp focus on the satisfaction of customers." Thanks to the many sales managers, salespeople, marketing managers, top managers of organizations concerned with the influence of the sales process on revenue and profits, and others for their feedback. Many of you reported your opinions of our first book to our publisher, ASQC, who passed them on to us. Others communicated directly. Regardless of your channel, the messages were clear. You said that the book broadened your views of total quality from technology to people and the systems or business processes you work with and within. Others said that the book broadened your definition of *customer* to include the person in the business process who receives your work, your input, and does something with it—

and that this person is important to the total quality of the sales process. And you said that the book created an acute—sometimes painful—awareness of the virtues and deficiencies of your sales process.

Others—particularly those with titles such as managers of quality or total quality management—complimented the book for helping to move their mindsets and the mindsets of their managers at the very tops of corporate hierarchies from the tangibles of product quality to the intangibles of process quality, and from a single function to the system of functions that make up entire organizations.

The authors addressed this broader viewpoint in *Bringing Total Quality to Sales* as requisite #8—process excellence. In the book, we stated that, "Quality transcends product quality to include business processes, the processes used to design, sell, deliver, and service the product. Poor quality within these business processes wastes both time and money, eroding competitive position, customer satisfaction, and productivity." More recently labeled *reengineering* or *business process redesign*, this concept has become the basis for *redefining the corporation*.

Those who commented agreed unanimously that our first book's good beginning needs other steps to expand the usefulness of the concept. "Show us how to use these principles" became a shared thread of your comments and the driver behind *Applying Total Quality to Sales*. Using narratives based on interviews with top executives, sales managers, quality managers, and others, the book demonstrates how five companies of various sizes and with disparate missions and markets applied total quality to sales. Not to the sales techniques used by salespeople, mind you, but to the sales process within which salespeople function, or, in some cases, are prevented from functioning.

Each narrative displays considerable insight into the thinking of the interviewees and demonstrates the importance of the 10 requisites from total quality in sales put forth and defined in our first book, and, for at least two of the requisites, refined and expanded to reflect the mindsets of forward-thinking managers.

Those 10 requisites are

1. Require management commitment.
2. Evaluate managers by how much they improve quality.
3. Move your mindset away from manufacturing and into the intangibles.
4. A sharp focus on the satisfaction of customers. (*Satisfaction* is too benign a concept for today's world and implies a short-term commitment. *Delight* is more dynamic and long-term; it is explained in chapter 3 regarding Xerox. Still more dynamic is *anticipation*, a decidedly strategic concept manifested by all the companies profiled but under a different banner. Therefore, the authors propose changing to: A *sharp anticipation of the needs and wants of customers*.)
5. Sell the differentiation of value, not price.
6. Sell service, create loyal customers.
7. Sell quality, raise profits.
8. Process excellence.
9. Communicate, communicate, communicate.
10. Train, train, train. (*Train* implies the imparting and productive use of existing knowledge. *Educate* expands the use of knowledge to include its creative application; it is training beyond the basics to application of the basics in new ways.)

Requisite #4—a sharp focus on the satisfaction of customers (and, by extension, the anticipation of customers' needs and wants)—permeated all the companies so pervasively that it had become part of the very fabric of the organizations from top to bottom. It seems impossible to single out one of our interviewees that is more committed to customers than the others. We could never decide, for example, which group of salespeople were more focused on total quality management—the auto salespeople at #1 Cochran, who live by the credo "value people selling people value," the order entry and tech support team members at Black Box who live by "customers come first," the associates at Xerox who are guided by "quality is the bridge to our customers," or others who live by other missions stated just as succinctly and pointedly. All are committed in their own ways, and all can point to the success of their ways.

Although all other requisites have been applied to some degree by all the reported companies, it became clear as the stories developed that precedence or emphasis of one or a few requisites is the norm. For example, we were more than impressed with the total commitment of Black Box president Jeff Boetticher, a living testimonial to requisite #1—management commitment. Boetticher and his manager of quality, Paul Leger, live and breathe total quality; they walk the way they talk, and this steadfast fidelity of purpose is a profound influence on and role model for employees, called *team members*. Both Boetticher and Leger constantly remind team members that *customers* (in the sense of *purchasers*) *come first*, and insist that team members be empowered to live by that basic tenet.

A rare customer complaint is resolved by Boetticher himself, 20 minutes after receiving it, if the line team member cannot resolve it in 24 hours or the department manager in four hours. If Boetticher is forced to resolve the complaint, he considers customer satisfaction first, costs second. His rationale, he points out, is cost-effective over the longer term: It costs five times more to find a new customer than it does to keep an existing customer.

Another anecdote reinforces that requisites #6—sell service, create loyal customers—and #7—sell quality, raise profits—are *lived* at Black Box. An order entry team member accepted an order at 4 P.M. Then, remembering that the fabrication department stops work at 3 P.M., found herself at odds with a company policy that *all* orders entered by 5 P.M. be shipped that same day. So she empowered herself to fabricate the unit, then had it packed and shipped, staying on the job until 7 P.M. to do so. Is there any doubt that customers come first with all team members at Black Box? Or that the CEO leads the way?

We were impressed as well with Xerox and its evaluations of employees based on improvements to quality as well as financials, supporting requisite #2. Rigorous and formal procedures for performance evaluations focus on quality of relationships with internal and external customers, not quality of products. An overriding philosophy is that the financials will take care of themselves if employees take care of the softer sides of quality.

Chester Howell, operations manager of Xerox's Pittsburgh District Office, is convinced that customer satisfaction isn't enough, that satisfaction is far too benign an emotion. Instead, he talks of customer delight, a feeling that is so powerful that customers want to do business _only_ with Xerox. A retired chairman of a Fortune 500 firm put forth a similar definition reported in _Bringing Total Quality to Sales_. He said, "People tend to hear total quality as buzzwords, as motherhood. So I go a second step and give my definition—to do everything so well that the customer wants to give us _all_ of the business. He wouldn't do business without us."

Delight defined another way means _meeting needs of customers that customers aren't aware they have_—new products, features, or services that customers have yet to experience and wouldn't know how to ask for, yet somehow subconsciously tie into their definitions of value. These under-the-surface needs and a supplier's anticipation of meeting them form perhaps the third level of customer awareness: The first is meeting standards, and the second is meeting expressed or known needs.

Moore Business Forms is expanding its focus on quality from its plants to its sales and support functions, a clear demonstration of requisite #3—move your mindset away from manufacturing and into the intangibles. Today, the company's quality efforts embrace all product and service offerings and the business processes that support its ability to delight customers. In part, this has been achieved through quality training across the breadth and depth of the entire firm. Every associate—in all functions and in all levels—receives a minimum of three days of quality training.

In managing for sales quality, four initiatives combine to focus on supporting the sales process: competitiveness through learning; error management; quality as a selling tool; and systematic support for sales quality. The four initiatives recognize that total quality starts and ends with salespeople, the account managers who interface with their customers—executives, key decision makers, influencers, purchasers of products and services, and users.

And many of the actions, that is, programs that support those initiatives, zero in on improving the sales process, in turn raising the effectiveness of salespeople and the efficiency of the processes by which the company delivers value to its customers.

Profiling an auto dealer in a book about the total quality of sales might seem to stretch the bounds of credibility: Probably everyone over the age of 25 can spin a tale of horror about purchasing a car, with the car salesperson playing the very caricature of unsavoriness—the exact opposite of quality. Rob Cochran, the young and forward-thinking president of #1 Cochran, a large auto superstore, changed this stereotype by changing the sales process and the attitudes of his people. His main focuses are on communications, requisite #9, and training, requisite #10, to sell the differentiation of value, requisite #5. Walk into any one of the three Cochran superstores, and you'll be greeted by a friendly receptionist who will ask about your interests, and then introduce you to the salesperson who is most qualified to discuss them with you in a calm, objective manner. You'll be shown cars in a clean, carpeted showroom; visit the service department and meet the service manager in charge of the vehicles that interest you; and be taken for a test-drive in an immaculate demonstrator. There's no pressure to buy, no hype about features, no sly come-ons about the deal-of-the-decade. The entire package radiates concern for putting the customer in the car of his or her choice with the least possible hassle and lowest possible cost.

The reason is simple: Cochran people, organized in sales/service teams, live by the tenet that Rob Cochran lives by: *Value people give people value.*

Construction Tool Services, like #1 Cochran, focuses on selling the differentiation of value and service to create loyal customers. This small distributor of tools, most of which are commodities, uses focus groups, informal meetings, and other techniques to define, as sharply as possible, what customers want and will pay for. And, faced with increased competition from the large do-it-yourself stores, Paul Connelly, the president of Construction Tool Services, has been the driver behind formation of a group of 61 distributors that not only buys from manufacturers in bulk for lower prices, but also calls on manufacturers for extended training of all their inside and outside salespeople, increasing their value to customers.1 Add to that the extraordinary spirit of teamwork exhibited by the firm's employees and the computerization of inventories, pricing, and deliveries that streamlines and goof-proofs the sales process, and it's no surprise that Construction Tool Services was honored for significant improvement in reaching the goals of total quality management. The award is the second highest bestowed by the Pittsburgh Chamber of Commerce.

The question often posed to us is: "Which of the five companies is most committed to total quality in sales?" The answer is, "all of them." We understand that all can't be "most committed," yet all *are* in their individual ways. The corollary question: "Which approach is most effective, has yielded the best results?" The answer again is, "all." The process of applying total quality to sales is unique to each company. As Jeff Boetticher of Black Box said after studying the processes offered by consultants and adopted by several other firms, "We needed to put a Black Box spin on the process if it is to work best for us." Barbara Riggs of Moore Business Forms said it differently: "Our total quality process fits us better than it could fit any other organization. Our processes and culture are uniquely ours." Paul Connelly of Construction Tool Service said it this way: "Sure, we're different than our competitors; that's what makes us better. So we need a total quality process that's better too, because it is our own."

Although the spin is unique to each company, it invariably builds on the accepted, effective processes each company already has in place; none of the people interviewed are willing to throw the baby out with the bathwater.

A main purpose of total quality management is to create the culture envisioned by the top manager, the organization as *seen* by the top vs. the organization as it is. The vision, to be workable, must be realistically attainable, in tune with human nature. That's why the goals of Jeff Boetticher's dozen or so measurements of customer satisfaction are never 100 percent; it's not realistic to expect perfect performance that is measured by an imperfect measurement system.

This brings us back to requisite #1—management commitment. It's impossible to bring or apply total quality to sales (or any other function, for that matter) without management commitment. It is the *go, no-go* requisite, as was proven by all of the reported companies. The CEO of Xerox, for example, continuously reinforces his commitment through speeches and personal supervision of corporate audit teams. Managers at district offices live by his mission, and most district offices employ a manager of quality who is focused on the sales process.

A recent message by the president and CEO of Moore Corporation set forth three priorities: customer satisfaction, quality, and asset management. Moore quality professionals are ensuring that all three priorities—with quality as the centerpiece—are integrated into the daily work of all associates. His clear, unequivocal mission reinforced the sense of urgency depicted in an earlier speech by a top corporate executive who said, "The quality train is leaving the station, and you'd better be on board."

Jeff Boetticher, Paul Connelly, and Rob Cochran are more visible to all employees and lead their smaller organizations by day-to-day example. Like their counterparts in larger organizations, their missions are communicated through formal and informal channels, and by actions.

A trait shared by all top managers is their ability to think strategically and in terms of dynamic systems and processes that span entire organizations. It's encouraging to note that the interviewees don't fit the mold of American managers who are often derided for their narrow, short-term views. Instead, they stay the total quality management course because they know the course is best over the long haul. They also recognize that focusing narrowly on a product,[2] a function, an event, or even a single business process can be self-defeating; that a view of the entire business as a system is needed for the dramatic and lasting results that are expected. So, the top managers we interviewed focus on the larger trends and relationships between, for example, external and internal customers. They avoid the *snapshot thinking* that traps them into decisions that affect, perhaps positively, one small part of their operations while, at the same time, affect, perhaps negatively, other parts.

All of which begs the question: Is a focus on the sales process too narrow, too confining? The short answer is, "Yes, it is." Still another answer might be that total quality starts and continues by way of the sales process, and that all other processes within the company are affected in some way. Therefore, the sales process is the logical starting point for applying total quality to all processes.

This is, in fact, the dynamics at the five profiled companies. Employees at all levels have moved their mindsets from production lines to key business processes such as sales, and from key business processes to companywide processes.

The authors would like to take credit for that concept, but can't. W. Edwards Deming laid the groundwork for this holistic way of thinking when he introduced the concept to the Japanese in 1950. He then wrote about it in his book *Out of the Crisis*.[3] And a number of top executives from GE's Jack Welch to Wal-Mart's Sam Walton have expressed the concept in their own terms.

It's fashionable these days to wring our hands in despair while decrying that U.S. managers lag woefully behind their Japanese and German peers in changing bureaucratic, inefficient, ineffective, mistake-prone processes too sleek, efficient, effective, and error-free processes. The case studies presented in this book prove that fashion can miss the mark. We who are concerned with the future of free enterprise and American capitalism should be thankful.

CHAPTER 2

CULTURE SHOCK ON THE SHOWROOM FLOOR

"'I'll be damned if I'm going' shouted Bobby Bluster, his round face even ruddier than its normal maroon, C-12 according to GM's code. It was now a C-16, cherry red with a touch of crimson. Bobby had been selling cars for just about the entire 31 years of his working life. He's an OK salesman now and was great once. He was great back in the days of starry-eyed buyers who wanted only to kick a tire and slam a door or two, when buyers were hooked when they smelled that uniquely exciting aroma of new interiors, fresh paint, and rubber yet to have turned hot on the road. Back in the days when making the sale—landing the fish, they called it then—hinged on reassuring the buyer that GM or Ford or Chrysler was still turning out the good stuff of the American Dream.

"The meeting had turned a bit ugly, not shouting-ugly, understand, but ugly nonetheless. I figured it might when I planned it.

"I'm sure that the 50 or so salespeople we employ here at #1 Cochran expected the same old meeting agenda: how we did last month, who sold the most cars, how many prospects are on the docket, what are the probabilities that they'd buy. Statistical stuff that's part of the business, part of everyone's job, and boring as all get-out for most salespeople, but not for me, Rob Cochran. I own the place—an auto supermarket that sells six lines of cars. Sales are over $300 million a year—they have to be to support acres of floor space, a thousand or so cars in inventory, and 350 employees from greasemonkey to me, the prez. Stats are a big part of my life, but I don't run the business based solely on them. Maybe I could have 10, 20 years ago, but times have changed.

"Yes, times have changed, and they've passed by Bobby Bluster. The poor guy hasn't figured out what hit him, why his old give-'em-hell, make-'em-smell salesmanship isn't working anymore, or at least not as well. He's confused, angry, frustrated, and probably taking it all out on the bottle and his family.

"One suggestion of mine set off his tirade. 'I think,' I said to the group, pulling together all the nonchalance that I could muster, 'that we should all learn to trust each other, work with each other more, be a team.'

"'What the devil is he talking about,' I could almost hear Bobby thinking. 'I work alone, always have, always will. If this young punk of a prez thinks I'm gonna share my action with the other salespeople, forget it. I'm an island, a fortress.'

"'I know that saying we need trust and teamwork won't make it happen,' I continued, hoping Bobby and the 50 others on my sales force were listening instead of rejecting. I barged ahead, 'So I've arranged for all of you to go on an outreach weekend in the woods. You'll rough it, and you'll learn to depend on, support, and trust each other by climbing rockfaces, hunting and fishing for food, and in general learning how to survive on your collective wits. You'll go in the same sales teams we've already organized. You can refuse if you want, and nobody will hold it against you. But I really think it would help our sales and up your income, so if you're thinking about not going, please give it some more thought.'

"Bobby wasn't the only salesperson to shoot from the hip and turn down the idea without so much as a 30-second ponder. We're victims of the 80/20 Pareto rule, and, like most businesses, I'm trying to break it. It's a prison, locking us into thinking that it's OK for 80 percent of our salespeople to be successful and in the program, and 20 percent not so successful and on the fringes of the program. So I wasn't surprised when another eight of our people started to throw up roadblocks. They ran the gamut from I'm too old, too out of shape, too set in my ways, and so on. Too bad, I thought, I'm committed to this, and I'll bet I'm the only auto dealer in the country that is.

"The meeting degenerated to pockets of discussions as people turned to each other to hash over the pros and cons of this novel, for them, approach to business. I let it go on for a while, and turned to my own thoughts. What are my motives? Why was I pushing so hard for change? Why did I reorganize my sales force and repair crews into teams? Was it working?

"My first thought was a story that involves Bobby Bluster and really set me careening down this new road to sales success. A few years ago a prospect walked into the showroom, was greeted at our front desk, and referred to Mimi, one of our younger and more successful salespersons.

"'Good morning,' said Mimi, extending her hand to the prospect, a middle-aged man with a family, mortgage, and car payments on a three-year-old Chevy he bought from us. 'What can I show you?'

"The prospect left an hour later, full of good ideas for his next car. He promised to return the next afternoon after talking the purchase over with his wife.

"He did, walked in the door, asked for Mimi, and found that Mimi was off the floor. She was taking another prospect for a test-drive and would return in 10 minutes. None of this was lost on Bobby Bluster, who immediately violated one of the cardinal rules of our sales process and, instead of filling in for Mimi until she returned, assumed complete control over the sales process just as if he had started it with this customer.

"'Hi, I'm Mimi's associate and can take over for her while she's out.' The operative words for Bobby were *take over.*

"Well, to make a long story short, Bobby can be pretty convincing and overbearing. He made the sale and never told Mimi about it. So Mimi, convinced that the customer had lost interest in a new car and didn't come back as he said he would, lost full credit for a sale and full commission. She might have saved her sale if she had followed-up the initial visit of the customer with a telephone call—that's our normal procedure—but she didn't, so she could blame herself to a considerable extent. She might have lost a sale three years down the road as well, because our customers tend to come back, a fact of which I'm very proud.

"This wasn't the only case of backstabbing that I was aware of in those days when backstabbing was a way of life in this business. I often wonder how many sales were lost because of it; I'm sure we lost a lot. Prospects don't like to be passed around; they like continuity, a familiar face. We weren't giving it to them, and I'll bet our customer satisfaction ratings suffered because of it.

"Continuity suffered even more by the turnover of salespeople. In this business—100 percent a year is typical, so, at least statistically, there's no chance at all of a customer dealing with the same salesperson over a few years' time. I wonder how many sales that cost us. A friend of mine bought a car from a salesman he liked and remembered at another dealership. A few months later he called to buy another car for his wife, asked for the salesman, and was told he had left. So he had to start the sales process all over again, from square one, examining his needs and so on. That's inefficient. In this case, a new salesperson was able to land the order, but it could just as well have gone the other way.

"Continuity is only one of our needs. Others run much deeper. Perceptions of value, honesty, and integrity in our business tend to be pretty shaky. Customers think of our salespeople—not only ours, but all of them in our business—as enemies, out to gouge customers instead of helping them select the right car at the right price. Service departments are also viewed suspiciously as high-priced and incompetent. Everyone I know has a horror story to tell that knocks the dealer, yet the dealer is in the best position of anybody to be the lifetime source of transportation for drivers of all ages and tastes.

"So we reorganized, changed the sales process and how salespeople are compensated, and changed the culture. It's all wrapped in *quality* and *value* as we've defined those terms."

"The Bobby Bluster story never should have happened, and never would have happened, if our salespeople were really looking out for each other instead of looking out for themselves.

"'But it's so *typical*,' said one of my sales managers, 'that kind of behavior . . . and there are hundreds of variations of the same theme . . . is part of the business.'

"'How do we change it?' I asked, 'because we need to if we're to survive. We absolutely must find a way to behave in ways that tell the customer that we're vitally interested in his or her buying the right vehicle at the right price. We can't afford to employ salespeople or anybody else who signal that the customer's needs are secondary to the commission.' That set off a brainstorming session that lasted for half a day, then picked up for another full day. It led to a number of actions that are totally coordinated into what we feel is a complete plan. It will unfold over years, and, in fact, if we're smart, it will never end. We now know that total quality management is a continuing, continuous process."

"'Our goal is simple,' I said to the assembled managers during one brainstorming session. 'It's to change our culture to be totally sensitive to customers' needs and wants, not to ours. I want everyone so sensitive to those needs and wants that two things happen—customers keep coming back and refer us to their friends. And our good employees don't ever leave, or, if they do, it's not because business is bad or we're treating them unfairly.'

"'We need a slogan,' suggested one manager, 'a rallying cry. I know slogans don't change cultures, but getting one is a good way to involve everyone right at the beginning. We can run a contest.'

"'Good idea,' I said, 'but maybe a bit too early in the game. Let's discuss our values, what we stand for now, and what we'd like to stand for in the future.'

"We agreed that what we stand for is *value*, and that we've done a pretty good job of hiding that stand from buyers and employees. We agreed that we'd like to stand for value even more solidly and surely more visibly in the future. So we set out to define value in this business with such a poor image for providing it, and landed on six supporting ideals.

- *Honesty* displayed through straightforward actions and communications with everyone.

- *Quality* achieved by doing the right job right the first time.

- *Courtesy* shown through personalized service that responds to people's needs and wants.

- *Promptness* valued through the timely execution of requests and responsibilities.

- *Cleanliness* displayed by a clean, safe environment and professional personal appearance.

- *Consistency* maintained by everyone keeping the same high standards every day.

"Only after we were sure of our supporting ideals did we run a contest for a slogan to which all employees could subscribe. We got dozens of suggestions before we decided on:

Value people give people value.

"Our task as managers was to communicate our definition of value—the six supporting ideals—not only with words, but more importantly by being absolutely certain that we lived them every day. We'd always walk the way we talk, which is the best way to communicate a culture. We also held employee meetings during which we explained our mission and asked for suggestions. Based on them, we made some pretty big changes that work together to change the entire process of selling and servicing cars at my superstores.

"I wish I could talk about the changes separately, but frankly they work together and affect each other so much that I have to lump them. We reorganized our sales teams into groups of six and eight salespeople, with the old-timers who we classified as *resisters* spread among the younger people so they couldn't band together and slow our progress with the strength of a cohesive organization. Each team elected a leader who is responsible for the team's performance and behavior, including willingness to move with the program. The team leader can be dethroned anytime by a majority of the other members, so the whole structure is democratic and requires everyone to be involved.

"Recognizing that it's impossible to separate service from sales and that good service translates directly to higher sales, we organized our service people into teams that specialize in a single line of cars. We have a Cadillac team, an Infinity team, and so on for our six lines.

"Then we changed the compensation system. Our salespeople are still paid the standard commission at the time a car is sold, and, in addition, are paid a smaller commission two and three years after the sale. We think that our deferred commission schedule does two things for us and for our salesperson.

"First, salespeople can project a guaranteed income of some level down the road, something that wasn't possible before. And they can build up that guaranteed income to a level that offers some security. With that in mind, they tend to stay with us, because the deferred commission isn't paid if they leave. They also tend to follow-up the sale more conscientiously because the prospect of staying with us also adds importance to repeat sales.

It all adds up to greater continuity, consistency, and security. And the result: A significant rise in our customer satisfaction indices, and with it our market shares.

"Service people have a stake in the deferred compensation. They are made aware of the importance of service to repeat sales, and the importance of repeat sales to profitability and everyone's income.

"The sales team also benefits. Part of the immediate and deferred commission accrues to a special account shared at the end of each quarter by every member of the team. I think that this change slows down the backbiting of the old days more than any other change we've made."

"I'd guess by now you're wondering what happened on the outreach program and to Bobby Bluster. Well, all, except one, of our salespeople went on an outreach, and she declined for health reasons—legitimately, I think. Bobby went, as did the other oldtimers, some of them grumbling. I didn't mind; I knew this was a big step for them.

"The outreach was a big success. We got to know each other much better and to trust each other as a team. One of our salespeople, a former football star afraid of heights since childhood, walked across a fallen log that bridged a ravine 50 feet deep. The experience changed his life. He's more confident and relaxed, a much better person all-around but especially on the job. He's gone from a mediocre to a top performer.

"Our sales process has changed forever and for the better. Most of the teams really work as teams, selling cars to buyers who are very pleased with the attention they get without any pressure to buy on the spot. The service people are also pitching in to satisfy customers, not just fix cars, a broader perspective to help us be successful over the longer term. Everybody's income is up along with our customer satisfaction ratings.

"What happened to Bobby? He was one of four salespeople who just couldn't swing with all the change going on. He submerged deeper into the bottle, and it began to show in his work and at home. I heard he was on the ragged edge of a divorce. After a bit of prodding on my part, he finally left the firm and, last I heard, was selling cars at a small dealership, giving customers the *kick 'em, smell 'em* treatment that he knows so well and just can't shake. Who knows, maybe there's still room for the Bobby's of the world at some dealerships. *Not at mine!"*

3

QUALITY AND THE UPS, DOWNS, AND UPS AT XEROX

Chester Howell was in a reflective and pensive mood. The manager of business operations at Xerox's Pittsburgh District chuckled as he relived his 20-year career and how Xerox moved from up, down, to up again during that time. "The first up hinged on big doses of hard work to get our new products, copiers, accepted by businesses accustomed to carbon paper copies. Hard work was accompanied by the serendipity of being left alone by other companies that could have been our competitors," he said. "But the down and second up hinged on quality. We fell from the heights of business success to the bottom, then rose like Phoenix from the ashes of despair, all because of quality, first not-so-hot, then the best in the business.

"Everybody remembers the blue ink story," he continued, "when customers back in the fifties and sixties complained that our copiers wouldn't pick up blue ink. So our sales and service people told them to use pens with black ink instead. Maybe it was the ultimate in customer turnoffs. It certainly branded us as insensitive to customers' needs, and, eventually, helped erode our competitive position.

"This insensibility was a terrible way to run a business, and I can defend it only by saying that it seemed like the right thing to do at the time. Back then, we were the only game in town with a process—document copying—that was becoming more and more key to our customers' businesses as they entered the age of information. Everybody wanted our copiers simply because they outperformed any of the other copying methods—carbon paper, mimeograph, ditto ink, scribes. And the only way to get a Xerox copy was to rent a Xerox copier.

"Sales and profits grew. A quick glance at our operating statement said loud and clear that we were obviously doing the right things, when in fact we weren't.

"We were doing a great job measuring our financial performance and making the mistake of thinking that it also measured our performance as a business. We weren't measuring customer satisfaction, and, if we had, I've no doubt that it would have triggered an alarm heard 'round the company.

"Not paying attention to customer satisfaction opened our markets to foreign competitors. Somehow they could see the handwriting on the wall more clearly than we could. They saw the subtly smug attitudes of our salespeople that comes with being the only game in town, a take-it-or-leave-it approach to sales that, over the longer haul, can only create animosity, not the friendly, win-win, long-term relationships that build businesses.

"They saw that we were making copiers that broke down regularly, and that we were *fixing* the problem by dispatching an army of service technicians to the customer's site. Don't get me wrong . . . we saw this too, but we were running our business by the bottom line, and the service department was a significant contributor not only to our expenses, but also to revenues and profits.

"Our customers were evaluating us differently and not anywhere near as favorably. They wanted salespeople who would really dig in and get to know their business and its needs for copiers. They wanted machines that operated reliably, not long-term and expensive relationships with our service technicians. They wanted other suppliers of copiers, and the Japanese heard the call.

"The rest is history. Our market share dropped from 82 percent to 41 percent in only six years. And the corporation's return on investment (ROI) dropped to an unsatisfactory eight percent.

"'We had taken our eyes off of the customer,' said our CEO at the time, David Kearns. The blue ink–black ink story verified the truth of his statement, and it became infamous, not only among our external customers but also among our employees. I'm certain there were hundreds of similar stories.

"Our employees reacted to our loses as you might expect—with shock, disbelief, and anger. Once those emotional responses were brought under control, we reacted more positively with programs that would help us regain our lost markets. Benchmarking with the best in the business became commonplace, and we brought the company up to the highest standards in such parameters as product lead time and unit manufacturing cost. We formed a partnership with our unions that recognized the need for all of us to cooperate in order to survive.

"And we established a focus on quality that, I feel, was the standard of our industry at the time, and remains the standard today. The focus was set during a 1983 meeting of our 25 top executives, and it led to a quality policy that became a consensus throughout the company. That policy positioned quality as our driving force and was stated so succinctly and clearly that the consensus was almost inevitable: 'Xerox is a quality company. Quality is the basic business principle for Xerox. Quality means providing our external and internal customers with innovative products and services that fully satisfy their requirements. Quality improvement is the job of every Xerox employee.'

"I love the way our policy is worded. *Quality* appears in every sentence. Quality improvement is *the* job of every employee, not *a* job, or part of the job. It is *the* job."

TOTAL QUALITY MANAGEMENT SPEARHEADS THE TURNAROUND

"Total quality management—called *Leadership Through Quality* or *Leadership Through Quality at Xerox*—was phased in throughout the company beginning in 1985. It is a strategy for cultural change that enables and empowers every Xerox employee to meet customer requirements, achieve business priorities, and improve continuously. It also guarantees that employees have the right tools and processes needed to implement that strategy.

"Leadership through quality focuses on every part of the business, as it must, and the results have been more than impressive. Defect rates in our equipment have plunged from approximately eight percent to 0.03 percent. Our eight percent ROI rose to 14.1 percent in 1991, 14.6 percent in 1992. Revenue per employee jumped from $30,000 in 1972, when we had 100,000 employees and $3 billion in revenues, to $163,000 in 1992, when we had 110,000 people booking $18 billion in revenues. The price of our stock went from approximately $37 a share in 1991 to $84 a share in 1993, and we've regained almost all of the market share we lost to competitors.

"The numbers are impressive, and I wouldn't minimize them for anything. I also don't want to repeat the mistake of defining our business with those numbers. I feel the reorganization and coordination of our sales and service functions, and how we grade ourselves, are equally impressive and worth a closer look.

"We reorganized in 1988 into 65 districts in the United States, each managed by a partnership—we call it The Partnership, as if it were the only one around—of sales, service, and business operations. Every management employee in the district is compensated with bonuses tied to four common goals shared by every employee in the company.

- Revenues and profits
- Customer satisfaction

- Employee satisfaction
- Process management

Revenues and profits are self-explanatory, and, in my view, are the results of the other three goals. So, let's discuss them in some detail as the goals relate to the sales process, and the sales-service continuum."

Delighting the Customer

"I like the word *delight* when it comes to customers. In my mind, it goes far beyond *satisfaction*, the word that's so much in vogue today. *Satisfaction* to me has a ring of the past to it—the customer is satisfied with our performance on the last order and, based on that satisfaction, will look upon us favorably for the next order, maybe so favorably that he or she will want to do business with us.

"*Delight*, on the other hand, has a ring of the past and future to it. It takes place when customers are so happy with our performance on the last order that they *need* to award us the next. Maybe I'm describing the difference between *want*, a fairly passive emotion, and *need*, an emotion that cries for action.

"The difference is reminiscent of the chairman of a major corporation who often said that it's possible to create a competitive advantage so great that one company can capture *all* of a given market. What's needed for that to happen, he explained, is to do everything so well that the customer wouldn't or can't do business without us.

"To demonstrate that such an ideal is realistically attainable, he asks if it's possible to buy a VCR in the United States that isn't made by a Japanese company. We can't. The Japanese electronics firms, working together as one company with a single sales objective, hold 100 percent of the market with products and services that are world-class in cost, and that are sold—conveniently—in countless outlets from department stores to discount chains.

"It seems that the Japanese electronics companies know about delight. They know that delighting customers requires a new way of doing business, one that involves every employee horizontally throughout our organization and vertically from top to bottom. We express our new way to delight customers with our slogan, *Quality is the bridge to our customers*, and with four primary programs, each supported and complemented by others.

- Partnerships with customers via Xerox customer requirement analyses (XCRA) literally demand that our salespeople know the complete needs of their customers for document control. Our salespeople know our business so well that they can relate customer needs to our capabilities, quickly calculate the cost of meeting their needs, and more. XCRA is the key to developing the long-term relationships based on mutual trust and respect vital to our continuing success, and to our willingness to offer a total satisfaction guarantee: we'll replace any equipment or system that doesn't satisfy the customer for any reason.

- Empowerment of our salespeople to meet competitive pressures on the spot, a move related directly to our greater understanding of customers' needs and how to translate those needs to specifications and orders.

- Partnership with vendors to create selling propositions that customers find most attractive. For example, we partnered with AT&T to offer customers a 10 percent savings on long-distance phone calls if they contracted for certain Xerox equipment for three years. Both Xerox and AT&T won with a long-term commitment.

- Renewed understanding of the sales process and how it leads the way to total quality and customer satisfaction.

Quality and the Biweekly Leadership Through Quality Meetings

"Our twice-a-month Leadership Through Quality meetings bring the principles of the program to company operating levels. The agenda for each meeting is set by the partnership, and usually includes five main topics. At a recent meeting, for example, we discussed progress toward meeting our quality principles, the toughest standards for being a role model manager, new hire training, quality improvement, and Customer Satisfaction Measurement System (CSMS) quality plan.

"But before I get into the details of our meetings, let's touch on some background. Every district was audited by corporate for quality—we called it the National Quality Audit. The auditors looked very hard at how we applied the principles of leadership through quality—training, strategies for improving customer and employee satisfaction, and much more. We were graded on each with a *not satisfactory, satisfactory,* or *role model,* the best in the company that other districts could emulate. Each manager was and continues to be graded the same way. For example, there are criteria for me to meet that could designate me as a role model.

"Each district also follows a very detailed business plan that includes improvements to all aspects of quality. In fact, quality drives the plan, not the other way around. The plan includes all the tools needed to improve quality in all its facets."

Ken Boston, the district's partnership support manager, is responsible for coordinating the partnership meetings. "We address two of the four common program goals at each meeting so that all four are discussed each month. We discuss the goals as related to and affecting the sales process and our salespeople.

"As Chester Howell, manager of business operations, said, revenues and profits tend to be byproducts of the other three. We look at them closely, though, by customer and for the entire district. And so do our salespeople. They are compensated with a salary and a bonus based on meeting or exceeding goals for revenues and profits. The bonus, for example, is lower for sales that are less profitable than established guidelines, a compensation scheme that encourages selling the value of our equipment.

"Selling value has never been easy, and it's not for the lazy, unmotivated, or noncreative salesperson—the kind we try not to hire. It's also impossible to sell value if the equipment doesn't include the features customers want and isn't supported by after-installation service.

"Our salespeople are empowered to set the price of equipment within guidelines and based on the value the salesperson sees the equipment offers the customer. That literally demands that salespeople know each customer's business and needs for document control as they relate to our entire line of equipment. Only then can our salespeople match needs to equipment and optimize their proposals.

"An interesting success story demonstrates this point quite nicely. During a recent routine customer survey—I'll get into our surveys in a minute—the people at headquarters told us that a local government agency had 20 copiers made by one of our competitors. The agency was considering replacing the copiers with new models made by the same competitor. Our salesperson went to work, studied the customer's document processing and other needs, and uncovered some important features offered by our equipment that the incumbent couldn't match. We sold the quality of solids and half-tones in the copies made by our copiers, and their capabilities to make two-sided copies and to automatically insert tabs—all functions that would help raise productivity at the customer's office.

"Then we brought in four demo units to verify to this customer that everything we said our equipment could do was true. The bottom line is that we landed the order based on value, at a price that was higher than our competitor's. Equally important—that sale opened doors at other departments within the government agency, demonstrating the power of customer satisfaction and networking.

"Customer satisfaction is always on our agenda. Chester has said that satisfaction isn't enough—that *delight* is the real goal. Call it what you want, it's a big part of what drives our business.

"Our customer relations group is responsible for listening to the voice of the customer. The results of surveys by phone or mail are reported in great detail. Trends are plotted and analyzed.

Disturbing trends are evaluated and the root causes identified, and, more positively, opportunities for sales—such as the government agency I just discussed—are uncovered. Then people are assigned to remove the root causes of disturbing trends and change them to opportunities, and pursue the opportunities that exist, closing the loop.

"Our Customer Satisfaction Measurement System (CSMS)— is a formal process with four elements.

- Post-installation surveys
- Periodic surveys
- Telephonics
- Roundtables

The post-installation survey arrives at the customer's desk seven days after we install our equipment. It's a simple questionnaire accompanied by a letter of thanks for the business. The periodic surveys start six months after installation and they proceed at random intervals. The surveys provide statistically valid data in a consistent format used throughout the company; our district, for example, can be compared to any of the other districts worldwide.

"Customers rank 32 items by *very satisfied* to *very dissatisfied*, with three more moderate rankings in between. Then they're asked to suggest ways we can be more responsive, where we can increase their satisfaction with us.

"These formal surveys, conducted by people at our headquarters in Rochester, New York, to help guarantee objectivity, precede less formal telephone conversations with customers, and roundtables attended by customers and our salespeople. All have had profound effects on improving the quality of our sales process.

"Strategies set by the district marketing manager play a big role in our sales process. Manager responsibility includes launching new products, sifting through data on customers to see who is and isn't using our equipment, analyzing the features of equipment offered by competitors and comparing them to the features we offer to uncover competitive advantages, and generally working with salespeople to understand how best to approach a customer.

"All this comes together in a four-step sales process that works something like this. Our surveys uncover vulnerable accounts and opportunities. The salesperson and marketing manager develop an action plan for each account. If it's a vulnerable account, the precise issues are evaluated and ways to correct the issues are put in place.

"We then examine opportunities more closely. We know, for example, when rental periods are coming to an end, and the volume of copies made on that equipment. Then, with only a bit more information, we can propose replacements.

"Step 4 puts the salesperson in motion. He or she calls and visits the customer, discusses needs and wants and how they've changed since the original equipment was installed, and submits a proposal based on bringing together needs and wants that our equipment meets."

"Has it worked?" asked Chester rhetorically. "Yes, it has, and we think very well. The corporate financial numbers verify it. So do the customer satisfaction ratings, up corporate-wide 38 points from 1985 to today. Our district is doing a bit better, I'm proud to say, with ratings up almost 40 points. Employees accept the program because they see how it benefits them. And customers—well, they see the benefits, too. If they didn't, we wouldn't be here."

CHAPTER

THE FUTILE SEARCH FOR PIXIE DUST

Jeff Boetticher is president and CEO of Black Box Corporation, a maker and distributor of data communication equipment such as local area networks and wide area networks. His views of total quality management today brand him more of a realist than he was a few years ago, when he began to move the company to total quality management in every department, beginning with those most closely tied to external customers, such as order entry and technical service.

"We were looking for the magic bullet, the pixie dust that would transform our culture overnight," he reflected. "We discovered, quite painfully and expensively, that there's no magical quick-fix to culture change. We didn't understand the emotional barriers to cultural change such as the feelings of seasoned people—what's worked in the past is just fine for the future. So, we charged ahead as if it were possible to erase the past and create the brighter future I envisioned. We sent our people to total quality management seminars, and they returned with note-books full of good ideas and their heads empty of ways to imple-ment them. They thought of total quality management as the flavor of the month that would soon be forgotten, after which they could get back to their *real* jobs. They didn't realize how commit-ted I was and that their real jobs were total quality management.

"Black Box managers also were suffering to some extent from the not invented here (NIH) syndrome. We think of our business as unique, so maybe NIH wasn't a bad syndrome to suf-fer from. Surely our business was and is changing, and we needed to discard the past and change with it. Cultural inertia just wouldn't cut it in our new marketplace."

"I was appointed manager of quality in 1989," said Paul Leger, "and told to make total quality management a way of life at Black Box. That was the mission; Jeff left it up to me to find out how to implement it. I studied total quality management as it is defined and presented by all the top gurus, and, try as I might, I found it difficult to combine the theories from the gurus and make them fit at Black Box. I had to ask, 'Are we that different? Are we unique?' The difficulty was taking those broad principles of total quality and designing them in ways that could be useful to Black Box. Then, we were offered a unique opportunity from a productivity and quality center operated by a large corporation.[4] I worked with consultants there for six months and *learned* a great deal about the tools used to create a quality culture. Immersed in total quality management, I learned a great deal about the quality process at several companies. As my storehouse of knowledge broadened and deepened, I came to a series of con-clusions that, in retrospect, were pivotal to our program.

"First, we needed to design our own total quality manage-ment process, one that put our own spin on the best parts of the processes developed by others and added some of our own. Processes designed by and for other firms just didn't fit us pre-cisely enough, and force-fitting them would be counterproduc-tive. It would mean throwing out the good processes and patterns that we had developed along with the bad.

"Second, the process had to be simple to become a way of life, communicated and understood easily and quickly. KISS—*keep it simple and straight*—became a rallying cry.

"Third, we had to look at our business through the eyes of our customers and measure our performance against their highest expectations. We also needed to measure our performance against our best competitors using the same performance criteria, again as defined by customers.

"And fourth, support from Jeff every step of the way is absolutely essential. Not lip-service support, but way-of-life support. Jeff and I must walk the way we talk; anything less would spell failure in a big way."

The Key: Measuring, Raising Customer Satisfaction

"We're a sales organization," said Boetticher. "I realize that all businesses can make that claim, but I think we can make it more convincingly than most. Approximately 70 percent of our sales consists of products made by others. While we select these products carefully on the basis of quality, availability, delivery, and other factors that enter into our equation of value, the fact is that we don't have direct control over product manufacturing. On the other hand, we can control the parts that we do manufacture. The bottom line is that we are a distributor, a value-added reseller, of most products we sell. The sales process, then, is in essence our business process and takes on new significance.

"We sell by catalog—almost four million mailed to customers each year. Customers call in orders—almost 1500 each business day—if they know exactly what they want, and our people take the orders. We immediately start the process of filling orders and shipping them; our policy requires shipping every order received by 5 P.M. the same day it is entered.

"Very often, however, customers call in to our technical representatives and ask what they need for a certain application. Customers called almost 350,000 times in 1993, slightly 1500 calls a day, about the same number as call in to place an order.

They call to explain, for example, that they have one brand of personal computer, another brand of printer, and several types of personal computers to connect. They ask us what's needed to make the equipment work together. Our technical service and order entry people must know the answers to some very offbeat questions. One customer, for example, called the day before the Super Bowl. Desert Storm was in full swing at the time. As a result, security at the football stadium had been improved, but the stadium managers were having problems getting the additional security to work. The customer called us late Saturday evening, and we were on the phone until late Saturday troubleshooting to determine if the problem was in the electronic Black Box or elsewhere. Finally, the problem was found in the computer-maker's equipment, and the additional security for the stadium was quickly up and running.

"It's this kind of passion for satisfying customers that we want as part of the lifestyle of every team member. It's important that we have this passion because looking down at us from an airplane at 40,000 feet, we look like any other manufacturer/distributor. The difference is inside the buildings—our people and their mindsets."

Customers Come First

"Our sales process is for all intents and purposes our business process," continued Boetticher, "and the process is quite simple when you map it out. There are only three steps—enter the order, ship what's ordered on time, and collect the money. I often ask myself: 'If this is so simple in concept, why is it so simple to mess it up?' It seems like plain common sense, yet, as some sage said many years ago, common sense is not very common.

"The most basic of common sense is that 'customers come first.' I've tried to impress that simple truth on all of our people and to live by it every day in every way—to literally insist by my actions and policies that all my people live by it as well. The way customer complaints are handled is a good example. Line people are empowered to resolve complaints; if they can't or don't resolve a complaint for any reason within 24 hours, it is bumped up to department managers who must resolve it in four hours. If they can't or don't, the complaint is bumped up to me, and I resolve it in 20 minutes, guaranteed.

"We've established standards that we feel lead to customer satisfaction and that are used to measure performance. They're pretty basic to any sales organization and can be charted along with the responsible department, actual performance, and goals." See Table 4.1.

"We measure actual performance every day," continued Leger, "which of course gives us a clear picture of performance relative to goals over a very short time period. We also plot our trend one year to the next. Are we improving? Or are we standing still, or, even more unsettling, getting worse? To answer these more strategic questions, we plot the same data as averages for a month, for fiscal year-to-date, and for the past two years. Table 4.2 shows a typical comparison chart.

Knowing Customers and Competitors

"Each shipment contains a customer satisfaction survey form. It's easy to complete and send back," continued Leger. "It contains only five questions, a space for comments, and spaces for identifying the customer and suggestions for new products to carry. See Figure 4.3.

"Almost 1000 of these forms are sent to customers every day, and two percent are generally returned. In addition to computerized analysis, I read every comment the same day it is received. Poor comments are logged into the database and referred immediately to the responsible department head, who calls the customer that day and resolves the issue. I'm told of the resolution, also logged into the database. The whole process takes 24 to 48 hours.

"Each month, all negative comments are reviewed by the vice presidents and president, who must be satisfied with resolutions, or they take matters in their own hands. Also each month, the results of the survey are plotted on a bar graph and compared

Table 4.1. Customer satisfaction index.

Categories	Responsible department	Actual performance	Goal	
Domestic % of lines shipped by schedule date				
MTO purchase	Purchasing	100.0%	98%	★
MTO manufacturing	Corporate	98.3%	95%	★
Stock orders	Order satisfaction	96.0%	95%	★
Percent of stock items available at time of order	Materials	98.5%	97.5%	★
Percent of orders released by 5:00 shipped same day	Distribution	99.5%	99%	★
Percent of calls answered in low queue in Tech Support	Tech support	90.2%	90%	★
Percent of calls answered before abandoning	Tech support	98.0%	97%	★
Percent of calls answered within 20 seconds in Customer Sales and Service	Customer sales and service	91.4%	90%	★
Percent of calls answered before abandoning	Customer sales and service	99.0%	98%	★
Number of credit/invoice adjustments	Credit/order	0	0	★
Percent of product returned vs. gross billings	Corporate	6.4%	8%	★
Lab turnaround for in-house repairs (working days)	Lab	1	5	★
	# of categories achieved		12	

Used with permission of Black Box Corporation.

to the previous five months. So we have a six-month graph similar to Figure 4.2 of trends that very accurately reflects our overall daily performance."

Boetticher said, "We also complete a different kind of survey each year, one that asks all of our customers to rank the importance

Table 4.2. Customer satisfaction index, comparison chart.

Categories	Responsible	Average for month— Aug. '94	Average for FYTD '94	Average for FYTD '93	Average for FY '92	Goal	FYTD achieved
Percent of domestic (MTO) purchased lines shipped by schedule date	Purchasing	93.7%	90.1%	76.3%	64.0%	98.0%	
Percent of domestic (MTO Mfg) lines shipped by schedule date	Corporate	98.0%	95.9%	90.1%	80.3%	95.0%	*
Percent of domestic MTS lines shipped by schedule date	Cust. sales and service	96.3%	95.6%	95.0%	86.5%	96.0%	
Percent of stock items available at time of order	Materials	99.1%	98.9%	98.4%	96.5%	98.0%	*
Percent of orders released by 5:00 shipped same day	Distribution	99.7%	99.6%	99.2%	99.0%	99.0%	*
Number of calls answered in low queue	Tech support	86.7%	88.5%	76.7%	n/a	90.0%	
Number of calls answered before abandoning	Tech support	97.1%	97.7%	95.2%	91.7%	97.0%	*
Number of calls answered within 20 seconds	Cust. sales and service	92.8%	93.0%	88.1%	87.9%	90%	*
Percent of calls answered before abandoning	Cust. sales and service	99.0%	99.0%	98.8%	95.7%	99.0%	*
Average number of credit/invoice adjustments daily	Credit/order	1.75	1.9	2.6	6.7 (ADJ)	0	
Percent of product returned vs. gross billings	Corporate	6.3%	7.0%	7.9%	9.0%	7.0%	*
Average lab turnaround for in-house repairs (working days)	Lab	5.15	2.6	6.5	10.2 (days)	5 (days)	*
						FYTD total	8

Customer Survey
Your satisfaction is our main concern!
Please tell us how we're doing.

We want to accurately record your responses. It would help us to do so if you would check the appropriate boxes.	Right mark ●	Wrong mark ✓ ⓧ ⊙ ◉

	Excellent	Good	Fair	Poor	Don't Know
1. The look and feel of the product(s) in this package is:	○	○	○	○	○
2. The performance of the product(s) is:	○	○	○	○	○
3. If this product has a manual, its instruction are:	○	○	○	○	○
4. The packaging of my Black Box order was:	○	○	○	○	○
5. The time it took Black Box to fill and ship my order was:	○	○	○	○	○

Comments: _____

_____

_____

Name: _____

Title: _____

Company: _____

Address: _____

City: _____

State: _____ Zip Code: _____

Phone: _____ Black Box Customer # _____

Suggestions for New Products: _____

_____

_____

Used with permission of Black Box Corporation.

Figure 4.1. Customer survey.

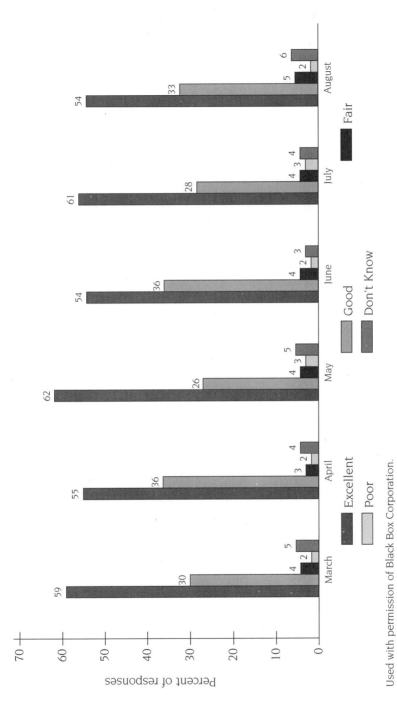

Used with permission of Black Box Corporation.

Figure 4.2. Monthly trends: Customer satisfaction.

of eight performance factors, our performance in each, and the performance of our best competitor in each. The survey combines absolute evaluations of performance with benchmarking and shows very clearly how well we're doing and where we could be doing better. We calculate a Quality Scorecard based on the rankings—the importance rating for each factor multiplied by our performance rating to arrive at our quality score as shown in Table 4.3, Column 5. That's compared to the maximum possible score shown in Table 4.3, Column 4. Subtract the maximum possible score from the quality score to arrive at our opportunity for improvement; the higher the number, the greater our opportunity.

"Table 4.3 and Table 4.4 demonstrate that a big opportunity for improvement is in the area of price/value, yet we rate somewhat higher in that category than our best competitor. I guess it's human nature to always be looking for a lower price and higher value. So we'll accept and understand both the positive and negative critique, and continue working to raise the value we offer."

The Velvet Brick

"I'm called the *velvet brick* by many team members," chuckled Boetticher, "and I deserve the nickname. One reason is the way I handle customer complaints, which we've already discussed. Another is the way I insist that all team members know our goals for the year and their responsibility for putting them into play. The goals—called SMART *Goals*—are always expressed as an acronym. This year it's SUPER, and the letters stand for

- **S**atisfy all customer needs in a quality way.
- **U**tilize skills to expand and grow domestic and international business at an accelerated rate.
- **P**roduce significant results in expanding product and technology offerings.
- **E**xceed all financial objectives.
- **R**ealize our commitment to making Black Box a great place to work.

Table 4.3. Quality scorecard.

(1) Factor	(2) Importance Rating	(3) Black Box Performance Rating	(4) (Col. 2 × 10) Maximum possible score	(5) (Col. 2 × Col. 3) Black Box quality score	(6) (Col. 4 × Col. 5) Opportunity for improvement
Product quality	6.6	8.6	66	56.8	9.2
Product availability	5.1	8.6	51	43.9	7.1
Price/value	5.0	7.3	50	36.5	13.5
Technical support	4.8	8.2	48	39.4	8.6
Speed of delivery	4.1	8.6	41	35.3	5.7
Ease of ordering	3.6	8.5	36	30.6	5.4
Ease of returning	3.1	8.2	31	25.4	5.6
			323	**267.9 = 82.?% of potential score**	

Used with permission of Black Box Corporation.

Table 4.4. Benchmarking against best competitors.

Item (in order of importance)	Black Box performance rating	Best competitor performance rating	Difference
Product quality	8.6	7.8	0.8
Product availability	8.6	7.2	1.4
Technical help	8.2	6.5	1.7
Price/value	7.3	7.1	0.2
Speed of delivery	8.6	7.6	1.0
Ease of ordering	8.5	7.7	0.8
Ease of returns	8.2	7.0	1.2

Used with permission of Black Box Corporation.

"Everybody gets a card, as many cards as they'd like, in fact, with the SMART Goals printed on it. Then I'll grab a fistful of pens and walk out among the team members and ask, for example, 'What does R stand for?' If the answer is wrong or an 'I don't know,' I give the team member a pen to write the correct answer. The member writes the answer knowing I'll be back with the same question plus a request to see the paper noting the correct answer."

The Move to Global Standards

"More and more of our business is coming in from customers outside the United States," continued Boetticher. "Canada is already a big customer, Mexico is growing, and I expect the European Community, already a significant factor, to grow rapidly as the continent pulls out of its recession. Japan is also big; this is surprising because we think of Japan as home for many of the products we sell. It illustrates that great service is valued everywhere.

"We're preparing for expansion overseas. We've already been certified for ISO 9001, the toughest of the ISO series to get.

It is described as quality system—model for quality assurance in design/development, production, installation, and servicing. Although this standard was developed in Europe, it is becoming the norm everywhere, and I feel it will eventually become the pre-requisite for bidding on many orders. That includes orders nego-tiated here in the United States.

"I view this trend of certification by an international stan-dards group, called *globe-able* by some folks, as the wave of the future. Buyers will look for certification before buying. They'll audit suppliers regularly. We've passed audits by such compa-nies as AT&T and Motorola, and the audits followed ISO 9000 and Baldrige procedures. I expect more of the same in the future, much more. In my view, every manager concerned with the future should expect the same."

CHAPTER 5

FROM PRODUCT QUALITY TO PROCESS QUALITY

"We're acutely aware of the need for applying quality to all operations in our business," said Barbara Riggs, manager, National Sales Quality, Moore Business Forms. "Total quality management means just that—*total*—from inception through customer fulfillment. The trail of information surrounding a business transaction starts with the salesperson discovering or anticipating a customer need. It ends with the salesperson monitoring customer satisfaction and working toward raising it to customer delight. In our company, then, that critical information trail can account for 80 percent of the cost of poor quality.

"Yet, like many companies, we had initially focused on product quality, the quality of our manufacturing operations. It's been referred to as *quality-in-the-box*. We recognized, however, the critical need to move beyond that singular mindset to a holistic approach that encompassed all of our business processes. A fundamental cornerstone was our belief that people inside the company build internal customer/supplier partnerships in order to satisfy and delight our external customers."

"Our sales process is generally pretty good," mused Walter Bridges, sales manager, Pittsburgh District. "It supports the efforts of our salespeople so that they can get on with the business of selling and satisfying our customers.

"Occasionally, however, the process breaks down, and it seems to me that the cause, more often than not, is a communications breakdown. I remember one episode that took place just a few years ago. I walked into our design department and found a very furious and vocal salesperson. Our inside designer wasn't too happy either. 'You messed up the design,' pouted the salesperson, 'and my customer is so disgusted that he'll probably give the order to one of our competitors. It's all your fault,' concluded the salesperson while wagging his finger under the nose of a design team member.

"The designer, no wilting flower, shouted back: 'It's not my fault, but if you're into finding fault, go look in the mirror. This design is exactly what you asked for, what you said the customer wanted. Here, look at your notes, your specs, and you'll see.'

"I have to give credit to our salesperson. He cooled off, examined the situation and his notes, backed down, and he and the designer put their heads together to come up with a design that suited the customer's requirements. The happy result was that we got the order, but only by a whisker. Cliffhangers like that I'd prefer to avoid. The unhappy result was that scenes like this were all too common and all too costly in terms of lost productivity and, I suspect, lost customers. The root cause—lack of total quality applied to the sales process.

"This particular scene was one of several of a similar kind that all unfolded pretty much along the same lines. The salesperson returned from a sales call with specifications for a new form, filled out a standard spec sheet, gave it to the designer, and ran out to the next sales call. There were either errors on the spec sheet or missing information. So the designer, pressed with a deadline and unable to locate the salesperson, either designed the form wrong because input data was wrong or interpreted the data to fill in the blanks, a risky business that too often leads to additional errors.

"I'm sure it was unintentional, but our salespeople were, occasionally, helping to erode the satisfaction of our customers and the cooperation and responsiveness of our designers. Obviously, that's not the situation the company wanted. So to reverse it we applied total quality to the entire company and to the sales function in particular. It was a cultural shift of huge proportions, and it's still going on. Let's look at some history. Moore Business Forms has always operated its business with quality in mind, but, like many companies, focused quality on manufacturing rather than on the less tangible functions such as sales. As Barbara mentioned, quality-in-the-box focused on tracking quality in terms of errors committed at our plants—errors such as poor printing, shipments of the wrong quantities, late or partial shipments, or shipments sent to the wrong address or customer. This focus gave us tunnel vision that literally prevented us from seeing the root causes. Many of these errors could be traced directly to the sales function, our sales *process*, and its lack of tangible measures. The process just did not allow our salespeople, designers, and others who supported the sales process to do their jobs right the first time. They were as frustrated with the process as the people in our plants.

"One of our initial steps on the long road of continuous improvement was to listen more keenly and formally to our customers. Surveys, focus groups in key locations, debriefing of salespeople—we marshalled all of these techniques to put us in closer touch with our external customers. In addition, we looked for opportunities to learn from the best. The criteria from the Malcolm Baldrige National Quality Award[5] provided one such opportunity. The firm adopted the criteria as a road map to benchmark the best of the best."

Train, Train, Train

"We also began a commitment to our customers and to our associates: Provide quality training to everyone—all 10,000 associates in the division. The first training step provided a conceptual framework about the principles of total quality management. Associates—from the top to the bottom, from the bottom to the top—learned a common language for communicating about quality and gained an understanding of their role in meeting customer expectations. The second training step provided analytical skills for seizing opportunities and solving problems. In addition, associates were trained on interpersonal skills and were provided with resources for working together in quality action teams. Teams are our way of demonstrating that every associate is personally responsible for total quality and that teamwork is the most effective method for continually improving.

"Sales representatives, designers, and sales managers all aligned efforts either within the sales function itself or cross-functionally across work processes. Salespeople and designers in sales offices, the president and the executive group in divisional headquarters, press operators and shipping clerks in manufacturing plants, all use the same FADE process to examine and improve the quality of products we manufacture and services we provide.

"FADE—an acronym for focus, analyze, develop, and execute—is an organized method that enables associates to focus on the right opportunity to address, uses quantifiable data to gain a greater understanding of the scope of each issue, assists associates in developing and implementing solutions, and tracks and monitors that solution to maximize benefits for our customers and our company."

The Four Initiatives for Quality in Sales, and the Actions That Support Them

"Leadership is appropriately the first of the seven Baldrige award categories," continued Barbara Riggs. "The word *leadership* connotes that a leader is, in fact, a leader because people are *willing* to follow. They're not merely complying; they're committing. There are similarities to quality. Quality must be much more than a directive from headquarters. Like leadership, quality—total quality—is a fundamental part of the culture in which associates must be willing to enroll their hearts, their hands, and their minds. It is essential for that culture to be part of how we do our daily work in every office in the company.

"As the manager for National Sales Quality, it was part of my responsibility to support that culture and to develop and implement strategies by which the sales organization could focus its improvement efforts. We addressed this by insuring that all national sales quality efforts were matrixed against four major drivers.

"First and foremost, understand the *what*—what's important to customers. Our sales quality efforts had to be in direct alignment with what our customers were identifying as the key attributes that drive their decisions to purchase from Moore. Second, our sales quality efforts had to be in direct alignment with the division's strategic business plan. After all, it's the strategic business plan that translates the voice of the customer into the organization's work processes. Third, our sales quality efforts had to be in direct alignment with Baldrige award core values and the seven Baldrige award criteria. The criteria served as a road map, our benchmark to look outward to excellence in the global community. And, finally, our sales quality efforts had to be measurable. A balanced set of measures is applied to all national sales quality programs. They include measures of the process and measures of the results both from the company's perspective and the customer's perspective.

"We focused our efforts by selecting four categories of sales quality initiatives: competitiveness through learning; error management; quality as a selling tool; and systematic support for sales quality. Each category has specific programs associated with it and each program is selected for its alignment with the four key drivers previously listed. It was a conscious, planned rationale because we recognize that quality starts with our sales associates, the people customers see first and equate most closely with our company. Our salespeople are stellar performers, and we want the sales process in which they work to be infallible!

"The imperatives work together; none stand alone as *the* key to success. Together, they form a cohesive whole with a focus that is squarely on the needs of our customers. We knew from day one that customers define quality, and we provide quality that meets their definition. That concept seems so simple, yet it is so difficult for many employees to internalize."

"The sales process was dissected into five steps to be certain that appropriate support was in place at each step," interjected Bridges. "The five steps to every sales process are: identify and meet with the potential customer; build relationships based on mutual respect and trust; learn and understand the components of each customer's business; relate our understanding to each customer's need for business forms, and provide them at competitive prices and deliveries; and monitor deliveries, quality-in-the-box, and customer satisfaction. These five steps contain a number of actions that are implemented by each salesperson based on his or her style and reading of the customer."

"We took great care in choosing programs," said Riggs, "because it's easy to overload any process. People lose focus when there are too many actions; it makes it increasingly difficult to see how daily work is tied to the main goals of customer satisfaction. We feel confident that we've focused on the actions with the greatest impact on our sales quality and that our sales organization can manage those programs effectively."

The Relationships Among Initiatives, Actions, and the Sales Process

"The four initiatives look at the entire sales process and apply to all steps," continued Bridges, "and align the sales organization with the strategic and operational plans of the other functions in the company. Some of the action items apply across the board, as well. For example, continuous learning knows no functional boundaries and neither does total quality assessment. Our salespeople know exactly what's expected of them and how they fit into the structure of the company as it is today, and how our top managers envision the future."

A few examples of these relationships among initiatives, actions, and the sales process are best shown in Table 5.1.

Table 5.1. Relationships among initiatives, actions, and the sales process.

	Identify customers	Build relationships	Learn customers' needs	Relate needs to capabilities	Monitor satisfaction
Initiatives					
—Actions					
Competitiveness Through Learning					
—*Continuous learning*, a basic tenet to assure that performance is better tomorrow than today. Focus is on prevention of below-standard performance and innovation to ensure improved performance.	X	X	X	X	X

Table 5.1. (*continued*)

	Identify customers	Build relationships	Learn customers' needs	Relate needs to capabilities	Monitor satisfaction
—*The Quality Advantage* (TQA) *and Quality Action Teams* (QAT), procedures for integrating training on the principles of total quality management into training of salespeople. For example, TQA comprises two phases of training: the components and common language of quality followed by the tools of application.	X	X	X	X	X
Error Management					
—*National Error Tracking System* (NETS), a proprietary database for reporting, in real time, errors, their costs, and time needed for their resolution. Root causes of errors are identified and prevention plans documented.					X
—NETS *Notes*, a series of newsletters that profile reports available in NETS and outline step-by-step recommendations for utilization of the data.					X
—*Error-free, on-time invoices*, a key indicator of customer satisfaction measured by setting benchmarks and tracking improvements.					X

Table 5.1. (*continued*)

	Identify customers	Build relationships	Learn customers' needs	Relate needs to capabilities	Monitor satisfaction
Quality as a Selling Tool					
—QAT *Training for Customers* interested in partnering with Moore. The focus of the training is on Moore's problem-solving methodologies. The results are a common platform for analyzing customers' needs for management of business information, and a shared commitment to addressing and meeting those needs.	X	X	X	X	
Systematic Support for Sales Quality					
—*Recognition* and rewarding extraordinary efforts by individuals and teams. Several awards implemented in the sales organization: Robert M. McGee, Jr. Award to the sales district for the best record for error-free days; Error-Free Reps Awards for salespersons who work for one year without error; You Make the Difference Award for any associates who, in the judgment of their peers, do right things right; and SAM Award, the highest in the company, for teams that contribute significantly to customer satisfaction and operational excellence.					X

Used with permission of Moore Business Forms.

CHAPTER

SLUGGING IT OUT WITH VALUE IN DISTRIBUTION

"Yes, I have a very clear vision for this company," answered Paul Connelly, CEO and president, Construction Tool Services, "and I'm confident that it's shared by all of our 32 employees. Our vision can be expressed in one sentence . . . to be the best value in construction tools our customers can buy. That implies a great deal. Customer satisfaction to the maximum, for example. The most helpful sales force in the business. Long-term and win-win relationships with suppliers and customers. And much more, all of which is in our strategic plan."

Paul Connelly grew up in the business of distributing construction tools to contractors. His company, Construction Tool Services, was started by his father in 1949, and he joined it in 1958, fresh out of college. "I've seen this business change like day into night during those years," mused Paul. "During my early years, steel was pouring out of the mills along the rivers that define Pittsburgh at what I'd guess was a record pace every year, with an occasional drop during a recession. The mills always needed to be modernized, rebuilt, expanded. Contractors—our main customers—were busy all the time, and we were here to help them.

"Then, in the 1980s, the mills started to slow down and then to shut down. Contractors shrunk in size, and many just folded their tents and moved out of town. Our markets changed from a handful of larger contractors to many more smaller contractors, all vying for work on smaller projects that were more commercial in nature than the old heavy industrial projects.

"Our competition started to change as well. The big do-it-yourself stores moved in, and with their buying power they could offer prices on many tools that we couldn't match. Some of the big national distributors of electrical equipment, plumbing supplies and other mechanical equipment added tools to their line to become closer to full-service. They took advantage of their national buying power as well, and prices hit the skids.

"It didn't take a brain surgeon, as the saying goes, to see the handwriting on the wall. The handwriting said to me, 'Change, or be run over.' So we changed, and quality, or total quality management, played the biggest role."

"Construction Tool Services (CTS) had never in its history stated its mission or prepared a strategic plan. Never. My father and I figured we knew this business so well that we could run it by the seat of our pants, and it was pretty tough to argue against that approach. We were profitable, growing modestly, and our employees were living a pretty good life.

"Then, in 1991, I realized that we needed a clear direction, with goals and the strategies and tactics to reach them. The changes around us were just too overwhelming to handle without some formal direction; our management style would no longer work. Two incidents stuck in my mind as the drivers behind this new way of thinking."

"I sold a good-sized order," said John Becker, CTS sales manager, "but was so unsure that the tools I had promised to deliver were in stock that I drove from the customer's site to our warehouse to check. I wasted about two hours because I couldn't trust our inventory control system."

"I did some quick arithmetic," interjected Paul, "and figured that this one incident alone cost the company about $100, simply because we can't put a salesperson on the road for less than $100,000 a year. Then I figured that our other salespeople—we have six—harbored the same mistrust of our inventory, so we were wasting lots of money, probably $600 to $1000 a week, which is big money to a company our size. On top of that, we were losing sales at the same time simply because a salesperson checking on inventory can't be calling on customers. I couldn't put an exact number on our losses, but I knew they were there, and I knew I wasn't happy with them."

"The salespeople weren't any happier," said John. "We're all paid on commission, and we're not paid to check the warehouse. So we were less productive than we could have been, and it showed in our paychecks."

Paul continued: "The second incident involved a phone call from a good customer who had called three times for a price on some tools and was told three different numbers. We just didn't have our pricing down cold. And we didn't record the prices we gave over the phone. Customers were confused, and we were losing business and long-term relationships because of the confusion.

"So we built a plan around value, quality, and customer satisfaction. The sales process played a key role, and the first thing we did was solve the day-to-day sales operations problems.

"I'm getting ahead of my story. Let's back up a bit. I realized that total quality management was the wave of our future and discussed it with my good friend Don McCain in Erie, Pennsylvania. Don runs a company similar to ours in type and size, Perry Mill Supply. Erie is a hotbed of total quality management, with the local chamber of commerce supporting training and a competition to be named the top quality company in the region. The Pittsburgh Chamber of Commerce now sponsors a carbon copy program.

"Don caught the total quality religion, especially the part about eliminating errors and cutting costs by doing the right thing right the first time. We talked about it, and his enthusiasm rubbed off on me and I initiated our own program.

"We started with—*What You See Is What You Get* (WYSIWYG)—to solve our inventory problems. Our people jumped on the WYSIWYG bandwagon, had a lot of fun with the word, identified 26 points in the system that could *lose* a tool, and fixed the problem. Today, we're proud of our new inventory control system. It's more than 95 percent accurate, and salespeople have learned to depend on it. There's no more running back to the warehouse to see if we can deliver what's promised. New tools and equipment are logged into the system within minutes of their receipt, not the hours or days it took before, so they can be sold almost as soon as we have them.

"I had heard about the Q-NET program sponsored by the Pittsburgh Chamber of Commerce. The purpose of Q-NET is to promote methods through which techniques to improve quality can be shared by companies throughout the Pittsburgh area and to promote training in the principles of total quality management. The training is supported by a grant from the Ben Franklin Foundation, an organization here in Pennsylvania that encourages the formation and growth of small businesses like ours.

"Training in the techniques of total quality management is obviously an important part of Q-NET, so I enrolled five of my key people; they're now true believers and the core of our efforts. They're training others in the company not only in formal programs, but also by their example, their behavior.

"About this same time I worked with six distributors around the country to form Evergreen Marketing Group and take advantage of our combined purchasing power. The group—now 61 distributors and 64 manufacturers—is working well and our costs for tools now are about the same as for the big do-it-yourselfers. And we've really expanded the availability of education and training programs, including some that I insisted be developed on the principles and need for total quality.

"We took other steps to improve our training and the competence of our people. I enlisted my wife, Dr. Betty Connelly, who is very experienced in the training field and active in the American Society of Training and Development. She showed us how to coordinate the skills of our people to create a well-oiled organization. And she convinced us that strategic planning and all of its imperatives—setting goals, measuring progress toward meeting them at least each quarter, and continuously examining our strengths, weaknesses, opportunities, and threats—along with other activities of the planning process are critical to success."

Selling Value: The Multiple Prongs of Planning

"Differentiating one distributor or one tool from another has never been easy," said Becker. "We try to differentiate CTS by the value we add to our customers' operations—value in the form of knowledgeable salespeople, accurate deliveries, fill rates way above the norm, and service after the sale.

"Defining how we add that value is the function of strategic planning. Our plan has five major principles, each supported by actions to convert the principles to reality. See Figure 6.1.

- Management commitment
- 100 percent customer satisfaction
- Leading-edge people
- Win-win supplier relationships
- Internal goals and strategies

"None of the principles or actions stand alone. Instead, they work together synergistically to direct the entire company, to establish the total quality management culture that we are convinced is so essential to our future. For example, the total quality management committee that supports the principle of management commitment can impact all the other principles in very important ways. Just one recommendation of the committee was to send two of our salespeople to train at Texas A&M University,

1. Management commitment
   - TQ committee chaired by president
   - TQ committees focused on pressing issues
     —remedial actions

2. 100 percent customer satisfaction
   - Customer advisory board
   - Actions to create win-win partnerships

3. Leading-edge people
   - Q-NET training
   - Texas A&M University training
   - Train the trainer

4. Win-win supplier relationships
   - Accelerate move to total quality management
   - Training in use of specific tools
   - Training to improve safety on the job site

5. Internal goals and strategies
   - Leadership in regional markets
   - Broadened customer base
   - Diversification of customer base
   - Broadened services

Used with permission of Construction Tool Services, Inc.

Figure 6.1. The components of value selling at CTS.

which we consider as an action under principle three, leading-edge people."

Following is a discussion of the five principles and their supporting actions:

1. *Management commitment*, demonstrated by involvement in and direction of the total quality management process. Says

Connelly, "One of my first moves toward installing total quality management as a culture throughout our company was to set up a total quality committee of five employees. I chair the committee and am a permanent member; other members are rotated every six months, so that every employee eventually participates. We address topics that cut across the company and affect everyone's job. For example, the expectations of customers and how well we're meeting them, the latest data concerning fill rates, trends in pricing, and our efforts at diversification.

"I also set up four teams for in-depth looks at some very pressing issues: pricing; rental/repair, a growing part of our business; image/awareness, how we're perceived in the marketplace; and new products/merchandising, our efforts to diversify and to alert our customers about them.

"A look at the operations of the pricing committee will provide some insight into how the committees function. We knew we had a pricing problem—I mentioned it earlier. So we appointed one person, Derrick Martin, to solve it."

"When I analyzed the problem to get a better handle on its depth and breadth," said Martin, "I found that the root cause was a lack of consistent data. A customer or salesperson would call in for a price on, say, 16 items. A day or so would go by and we'd get another call that revised the list, sometimes by only an item or two. Because of quantity discounts, delivery distances, and other factors, the new price could be so different than the first, there was no way it could be pinned on the changes to the order. The caller became confused—and maybe a bit concerned about our competence—and, at times, angry, especially if the price went up.

"We computerized our pricing. Everybody involved, inside and outside salespeople, in particular, can access the data. Prices, discounts, adders are all part of the system. And, when a price is given a customer, it's logged in the computer to make repricing consistent.

2. 100 *percent customer satisfaction*, through value selling, based on offering the products and services that customers say they want and will pay for. Only through value selling can CTS develop long-term relationships that benefit everyone, the classic win-win situation. "That, to me, is the essence, the very definition, of value," continued Connelly, "and the first step is to be absolutely certain that we and our customers define value in the same ways. To do that, we have to talk candidly to each other, and we do through our customer advisory board. Six customers from various segments of our market sit down with six of our people, including two from sales. The board meets three times a year at a site away from our offices so we're not interrupted unless there's an emergency. We remind each other that we're partners with the shared goal of creating win-win situations. Then we tackle some pretty tough questions—tough because they're purposely general and open-ended, and answers vary all over the lot: What is perfect service? Should customers be able to access our computers directly and check on the status of their orders? What are the major economic trends that will affect our businesses next year, in 10 years? How can CTS change to be more responsive to customers' needs? How high a value do customers place on our repair services? Should we offer repair at all? How can CTS offer highest value by balancing quality and cost? Is CTS flexible enough to be responsive quickly to various and changing needs? How important are just-in-time deliveries to smaller projects? To larger projects? How can CTS help to improve safety on the job? And others, all related to creating that win-win relationship that is based on mutual trust."

3. *Leading-edge people*, developed through the most effective training available. "I've already mentioned the five people we sent to Q-NET training and how they became the core of our train the trainer program," said Connelly. "We also sent two of our salespeople to Texas A&M University to study distribution. Texas A&M is considered the leader in industrial distribution, and our two employees came back after a one-week course full of

ideas that could be put into practice right away. I'm convinced the course helped make them the stars of our sales force, and I'm planning to send other salespeople.

"The training yielded benefits beyond helping two of our salespeople become the best in the business. It also helped uncover opportunities for improving the performance of our other salespeople. One, for example—a very good salesperson, by the way—was resisting the use of computers for inventory and pricing checks, and, as I've already mentioned, we moved to computers for these functions in a big way. So some tension built between management direction and personal style. I'm happy to say that this tension has been lessened by a better understanding of each other. I understand his point of view, while he now understands that computers help him be more productive. His computer phobia has almost disappeared."

4. *Win-win supplier relationships* based on a total awareness that suppliers and distributors are partners and can help each other be more successful. "The quality of our company is a direct reflection of the quality of our suppliers," stated Chuck Kotulsky, inside sales representative in Pittsburgh and team leader of the Total Quality New Products committee. "If their products perform poorly, then we, as the distributor of those products, perform poorly. The same is true of delivery and service after the sale.

"Black and Decker is one of our main suppliers," Kotulsky continued, "and is also a company on the leading edge of total quality management. Not long ago we asked its representatives to help us move more quickly into total quality management, and they responded with three, one-day training programs for all of our salespeople, inside and outside, including the few at our small branch in central Pennsylvania. I think the program was very instrumental in seating the principles of total quality management and customer satisfaction throughout our organization."

5. *Internal goals and strategies* that are supported by the principles of total quality management described earlier, and, in fact,

cannot be met and implemented without total quality management. These goals and strategies include

- Leadership in regional markets by locating branches where needed for optimum customer service

- A broadened base of customers in traditional construction markets and in recognition of the larger number of smaller contractors; diversification of the customer base to include manufacturers and hospitals in need of tools for maintenance, repair, and daily operations

- A broadened base of services to capture a higher percentage of each customer's business

- Diversification into manufacturing and/or fabrication to vertically integrate the company's offerings

- A more selective product line based on each supplier's willingness and ability to participate in the total quality management process and to be competitive in price, delivery, and after-sale support.

"I think the future of CTS lies in total quality management, that our future *is* total quality management," said Connelly. "All of our employees are involved, and all, or almost all, are committed and live the principles. Like other firms, even small ones like ours, there are a few holdouts who resist catching the total quality management religion. They will catch total quality management in time or be forced to play catch-up.

"CTS may be more of a sales organization than most companies simply because we provide only services and don't manufacture anything. So every employee is a customer service representative, including truck drivers, workers, and accountants. Employees' business cards printed with their title, function, and *customer service representative* remind them and our customers that the purpose of everything our employees do serves to satisfy customers by meeting their needs. Our focus groups are the most accurate ways I know of to identify customer needs. When we meet our customers, we're selling value that they want and for which they are willing to pay.

"Customer service extends to better management of inventory, pricing, shipping, repair, rentals—everything that surrounds a sale. Our people know the importance of these functions, and customers are responding to our improved performance everywhere in the sales process. That proves to me that total quality management is working for the company. It's proof to the Pittsburgh Chamber of Commerce as well, which recognized CTS for significant progress toward becoming a total quality business, the second highest award of three tiers. CTS is the smallest and only service business in the region that was so recognized, which of course is a source of fierce pride in all of our employees. And it all took place because we improved internal systems that directly improve the sales process and customer satisfaction."

CHAPTER

MEASURING THE TOTAL QUALITY OF THE SALES FUNCTION

The five companies profiled in chapter 1 through chapter 6 demonstrate that broadening the application of total quality management to sales and other soft functions that support manufacturing opens new opportunities for raising productivity and lowering costs. In fact, seizing such opportunities can be far more fruitful than confining total quality management to manufacturing: Manufacturing companies can expect that up to 80 percent of their costs of poor quality are caused by problems in such soft functions as sales. See Figure 7.1. Estimates of the costs of poor quality are as high as 100 percent for service companies. Yet many managers in both types of businesses remain focused on product quality, unable to broaden their perspectives to other functions. They are missing their most fruitful opportunities.

Total poor quality cost
$480 million
12% of sales

Estimated cost $ millions

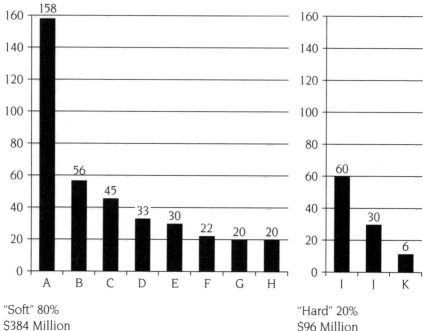

"Soft" 80%
$384 Million

A. White-collar rework
B. Product warranty
C. Excess inventory
D. Cash impact
E. Cost margin
F. Accounts receivable
G. Costly shipping
H. Overtime

"Hard" 20%
$96 Million

I. Blue-collar rework
J. Scrap
K. Field rework

Used with permission of Westinghouse Productivity and Quality Center.

Figure 7.1. Costs of poor quality: Of the $480 million per year wasted on poor quality, $384 million was derived directly from the soft functions shown, and $158 million of that from white-collar rework, to which sales is a leading contributor.

When total quality throughout a business is measured in the same solid terms as manufacturing is typically measured, it can set off a chain of events that sharply lowers costs and dramatically improves customer satisfaction and profitability. The chain can be initiated only if the business and its satellites are viewed as a unified whole, beginning with customers—only if the definition of customer is broadened to include the next person or function in the business process, as well as end users of products and services.

This shift in view from parochial to holistic—a shift in paradigm to frame it in current lexicon—can be extremely rewarding. A study of 50 divisions of a major company demonstrated that each 1 percent reduction in failure cost yields a 4 percent increase in operating margin. Preliminary studies of sales offices indicate that the 1:4 ratio is conservative when considering the sales, order entry, engineering, and other functions completed prior to manufacturing. The reason: the erroneous or incomplete information initiated by salespeople and sent to order entry clerks can cascade into manufacturing.

Despite its rewards, even top managers tend to resist this shift in paradigm. They often find it difficult to integrate the various pieces of their business into a unified whole. The difficulties are compounded for managers with narrower spans of control and influence. Division managers can be focused so tightly on the profitability of their single division that it is virtually impossible for them to consider if or how their day-to-day actions affect the mission of the corporation.

This type of focus was so ingrained at one major manufacturer that its top corporate managers formed a separate division to coordinate the marketing of products from several others as a *package* that customers had requested. The infighting and turf battles were so fierce and the short-term positions of division managers so unshakable that the coordinating division was disbanded after only a few years of operation. Losses totalled many millions of dollars.

Consider the plight of salespersons in such circumstances. In most companies, their span of control extends only to their immediate customers and is limited only to sales tactics. Their span of influence, if they are fortunate enough to work in a company that views its business processes as a continuum, might extend to order entry, design engineering, production control, manufacturing, and shipping.

The result is that salespersons find it extremely difficult to view the business as a unified whole in any but the most cursory ways. They either enter orders quickly to receive booking credit as quickly as possible, or procrastinate entering orders until the time is right or available. In either case, salespeople will overlook errors and omissions in the order, thinking they can be corrected or added later with change notices.

Perhaps their haste and carelessness are justified. Salespeople typically enter orders through a faceless name or onto an even more impersonal computer, and then have only the foggiest notion of the process after that. So it is not surprising that

• Salespersons tend to not understand fully the effects of errors in their communications to others. See Table 7.1 and Figure 7.2. Yet these errors can significantly erode profitability and customer satisfaction. A number of studies have shown that any given written communique contains at least one error of omission or commission. These errors can clog not only the sales process, but also processes downstream. Fixing the errors changes the process and initiates a chain of wasted money and effort that can consume up to 25 percent of a function's operating budget and staff hours, reducing profits and productivity accordingly.

During a recent assessment of a field sales office, an order entry clerk was asked to note the errors on orders entered and to record the time needed to correct them. In one month, the clerk noted 33 errors of various magnitude, an average of over one and one-half per working day. He wasted 10 hours correcting them. In another month he noted over 40 errors—was he becoming more

Table 7.1. An assessment of several field sales offices verified that the most frequent cause of rework is order entry. Note that of the 222 events only 24, change notices and reschedules issued by end users, can be attributed to end users; the 204 other events are generated internally (even end-user complaints), and many are initiated by salespeople. For example, proposal errors are typically the sole responsibility of salespeople, and many late shipments are caused by salespeople who misinterpret the needs of end users.

White-collar rework	Frequency	% of total
Order entry	51	23%
Late shipments	43	19%
End-user complaints	36	16%
Proposal errors	32	14%
Reschedule internal	21	9%
Change order end user	18	8%
Change order internal	15	7%
Reschedule end user	6	4%
Total	222	100%

Used with permission of Westinghouse Productivity and Quality Center.

tuned in to them?—wasting 12 hours to find and correct them, about eight percent of his time. Multiply these findings by 11 order entry clerks, and the costs skyrocket.

These figures are conservative because they tell only part of the story. At least three times that amount of time was actually wasted by the involved and peripheral employees: the time the salesperson spent to create the error in the first place, the time to find and fix it by the order entry clerk and the salesperson, and the time lost that could have been spent on a productive task, such as the next sale. And then there is the most important loss of all: The loss of customer satisfaction and competitive advantage due to delays in the process of completing the order.

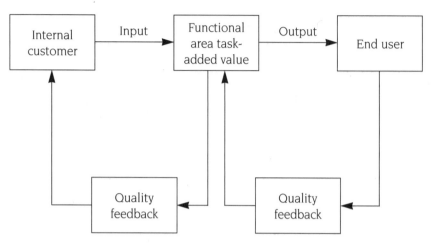

Used with permission of Westinghouse Productivity and Quality Center.

Figure 7.2. Expanding the concept of *customer* to internal customers (the next person in a business process) is necessary before an entire function such as sales can be assessed in terms of total quality. Every employee both receives and sends information. As receivers, they evaluate the quality of input. As senders, their internal customers evaluate the quality of their output. Countless dollars and staffhours are wasted when quality suffers in terms of timeliness, relevancy, and accuracy.

• *Salespersons—operating in a relative vacuum—tend to forget that they add considerable value to the product or service that they are selling.* They add a tangible aura of information around the product or service. If it is accurate and timely, the effect is positive; if inaccurate and not on time, negative.

Each salesperson represents a channel through which information passes from the company to the end user and from the end user to the company. The information flowing from company to end user takes many forms, from sales presentations to order entry to status reports. The information flowing from end user to company may range from anecdotes to formal surveys. The accuracy and timeliness of all have a profound impact on customer satisfaction.

For example, a study at Westinghouse revealed that at least half of all causes of customer dissatisfaction are related to errors, omissions, and delays in order entry. This finding triggered a study by a multifunctional team that plotted each step in the order entry process and highlighted troublesome steps.

The team then recommended, designed, and implemented a new computerized order entry system that enhanced the previous system with a sequence of menu-driven, interactive screens that

—Allow the salesperson to configure engineered products item by item, eliminating the need to transfer design data to engineering.

—Verify that the design is manufacturable.

—Suggest other configurations that could be less costly and more manufacturable without compromising the needs of the customer.

—Calculate price, including applicable discounts and shipping.

—Allow electronic transfer of funds for payment, and direct access by certain customers to both order entry and status reports.

• *With salespersons on the fringes of the business process, managers tend to forget that salespersons are their best sources of information about end-user customers.* Total quality management starts and ends with end users as well as internal customers and is driven by their real and actual needs and wants that are—or should be—communicated throughout the organization by salespeople.

Total quality management is a continuous, circular process that always begins and ends with end users who communicate with salespeople. See Figure 7.3.

Salespeople transmit orders and specifications from end users to internal customers in order processing, design engineering, and production planning, where small errors can cascade into major cost overruns (which the business will likely survive

Total Quality Operating System

Production Scheduling
- Production control
- Fabricating
- Finishing

Used with permission of Westinghouse Productivity and Quality Center.

Figure 7.3. Total quality management is a continuous, circular process that always begins and ends with end users (customers) who communicate with salespeople.

for some time, although unhappily and unprofitably) and erosions of customer satisfaction via delays and products that do not meet specifications (which the business is unlikely to survive for very long as customers move their business to competitors). These small errors are, in fact, erosions of customer service and profitability. On the other side of the coin, a study by a prominent consulting group concluded that an undifferentiated product can command up to a 10 percent price premium when supported by outstanding service.

Is Your Sales Function Ailing?

Look for the following symptoms, which indicate the need for total quality management of the sales process.

 • *The error chase*, characterized by a continuous need to hunt for and correct errors—whether misleading or missing information—in oral or written communications.

Case study: A customer service representative at one sales office was proud of his productivity. He was identifying and correcting an average of three customer complaints per day. We pointed out to him and his manager that the number should and could be zero. The representative blanched as he visualized the unemployment line—until it was pointed out that his talents were wasted on correcting errors and placating customers when he could be working on something productive, such as booking new orders or accelerating the completion of existing orders. Their viewpoints shifted, and both the representative and his manager set out to trace the sources and causes of errors and remove them.

 • *The overstuffed process*, characterized by too many steps involving too many people who don't need or want to be involved.

Case study: A step-by-step examination of the process for settling claims from customers for warranty work showed that the process required 32 signatures and 45 days to complete. Managers analyzed the cumbersome process by plotting its steps and surveying each of the 32 participants. See Figure 7.4.

The survey consisted of one question: Do you need to review or approve the paperwork? Only eight people responded *yes*. They were empowered with the authority and responsibility to settle claims in ways that were fair to all parties and that led to satisfied customers. The results: Claims were settled in 15 days, and the company saved over $3 million a year.

 • *The customer schmooze*, an extensive and/or misplaced placating of irate customers by salespersons and managers because

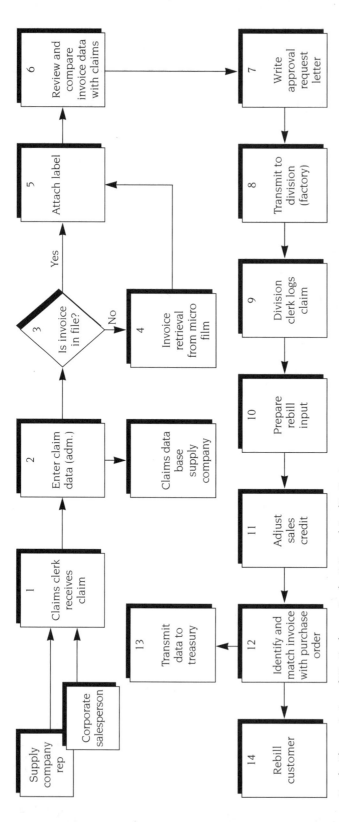

Used with permission of Westinghouse Productivity and Quality Center.

Figure 7.4. A multi-functional team plotted the processing of claims by end-user customers, highlighting loops, reworks, and other events that merely hindered the process and frustrated both end-user and internal customers. Claims were settled in an average of 6 weeks at a cost of $250 in time, regardless of the size of the claim. When claims clerks (Step 1) were empowered to settle claims below $500 that they felt were justified, most claims were settled in one week or less, and costs were reduced by 30 percent.

of missed delivery dates or poor product quality, unavailability of information covering the status of orders, and other conditions relating to the sales process.

Case study: The editor of a newspaper hand delivers a paper and a dozen roses to subscribers who call in and complain that their paper was not delivered. Customers are placated and the editor feels vindicated. But he is, in fact, misappropriating his time: He could ask an employee to deliver the paper, or, better yet, he could find and treat the *cause* of missed deliveries, not the symptom.

• *Misleading data and reports that make managers look good, even while the business is performing badly.* Measuring performance against standards that allow ample room for downtime, rework, and breakdowns in the business process is always misleading.

Case study: An initial assessment of a manufacturer in Hungary verified that, according to available data, product quality and on-time deliveries were excellent. Managers suspected otherwise. Further studies uncovered that the quality program was founded on delayed shipment of defective products to the Russians, one of their two customers, and on-time shipment of good products to the Irish. Their rationale was simple: The Russians evaluated performance using a 30-year-old system that had never been updated, so they rarely, if ever, found anything to complain about. The Irish, on the other hand, were more critical, and evaluated performance on standards that were far more stringent. Their complaints were both frequent and valid.

• *Narrow views of business processes,* the most pervasive and persistent symptom found during more than 60 total quality assessments of the sales-to-delivery process.

Case study: A division at Westinghouse operated under the delusion that on-time deliveries meant on-time transfer of products to shippers. Their typical response to end users who complained about late deliveries was to blame the shipper, angering customers. The solution was to negotiate guaranteed loading and delivery dates and times with shippers.

• *Evaluating the person, not the process*, typified by use of the conventional measures of performance described next.

Conventional Performance Measurements Focus Inwardly

The performance of salespersons, sales offices, and, to a limited extent, the entire sales function is typically measured according to these five ratios.

1. Direct selling costs equal total sales salaries divided by gross sales.

2. Sales dollars per hour equal gross sales divided by total hours worked.

3. Sales per salesperson equal number of sales divided by the number of salespeople.

4. Sales dollars per salesperson equal gross sales divided by the number of salespeople.

5. Average dollars per sale equal gross sales in dollars divided by the number of transactions.

There is no denying that these ratios can help companies identify outstanding and poor relative financial performance. The key words are *relative* and *financial*: The financial performance of a salesperson or sales office can be compared to others or to the average of all within the same company. And, if the appropriate data were available, it would be possible to compare performance with that of competitors. For example, an electrical distributor we assessed routinely compared its dollar sales per employee to figures for the entire industry published by an association that collects such data from all its members.

These ratios are almost completely focused internally, useful only to managers wanting to compare financial performances within the business. Nevertheless, the ratios are pervasive throughout many companies, and they rarely if ever provide feedback from customers or feedback on service performance to customers. In short, the ratios are not focused externally on customers, whether internal or end users. Therefore, their capabilities to add value to the business over the long term are very limited.

An internal focus can be dangerous to the financial health of any business. Xerox and Moore Business Forms are recent examples described in chapter 3 and chapter 5, respectively. When competitors eroded the imposing market shares that both companies held during the seventies and early eighties, their CEOs announced dramatic changes in corporate directions, along with renewed emphases on total quality management. The improvements have been measurably dramatic, and are continuing as their missions are reinforced.

Measuring Outward

Measurements in a total quality management environment focus outwardly on customers' expectations. Customers—whether the next person in the business process or the end user of the product or service—have expectations that are either met (for high customer satisfaction) or unmet (for low customer satisfaction). These expectations must be defined both qualitatively (what they are) and quantitatively (the ranking of their importance). Only then can sales and other strategies be defined along the lines of total quality management.

Expectations of customers—again, both internal and end user—cannot be defined by casual conversations and such open-ended questions such as, "How am I doing?" In fact, such surveys tend to lead to assumptions that can be misleading and destructive. For example, when production line workers at one motor manufacturer were asked, "How's your quality?" the typical answer was, "Great." The answer to the next question, "How do you know?" revealed the destructive, inwardly-focused culture prevailing at the business: "Our engineers say it's great!" The plant is now closed, a victim of prophesy, hunches, opinion, and guesswork (PHOG)—in place of facts derived from the marketplace.

Expectations can only be defined by properly designed and executed surveys that dispel erroneous assumptions made because internal people *know* internal customers so well, and salespeople and managers *know* end users.

Westinghouse managers *knew for sure* that the primary concern of salespeople about their company cars was engine size: six vs. four cylinders. A survey proved that engine size was not even among the top five concerns. Leading the list by wide margins were the number of available options and management's failure to consult each salesperson about specific terms of the lease. They were followed by untimely deliveries, unfair selling prices at the termination of the lease, and a failure to define billing and payment procedures.

Marketing managers at one Westinghouse division *knew for sure* that their customers were buying on price and technology. An extensive survey demonstrated that this was true for only a small percentage of buyers. Delivery and the immediate availability of applications advice were by far the most important buying criteria for over 90 percent of their customers. Knowing this, the entire sales and sales support functions were changed to absolutely guarantee the availability of a knowledgeable applications engineer at all times, and inventories were revised to absolutely guarantee availability of most products anywhere in the country.

The Four Measurable Imperatives

Surveys focused directly on the sales function tend to focus on four measurable imperatives: the timeliness, relevancy and accuracy of information, and the attitudes of employees. All were considered when studying the process of ordering and delivering a circuit breaker.

Customers were demanding just-in-time deliveries of circuit breakers in seven days or less from the date of order. An average of 22 days was needed, however, seriously eroding the competitive advantage of the business, and causing sales to be lost.

According to the division manager: "Thirty percent of all orders entered are incomplete, and over 50 percent of all orders are entered during the last five days of the month. I can only assume that salespeople are sitting on orders for days before entering them, and that they need to be more aware of the costs and problems created by orders that aren't written clearly and completely. For example, incomplete and erroneous information just adds to the load of product designers and slows down the process."

A team of representatives from the field and inside sales, factory marketing, design, and manufacturing functions was assigned to study the process and recommend ways to accelerate it. The cross-functional nature of the team eliminated finger-pointing and allowed each member to focus on meeting the needs of customers. Their first step was to plot each step on a flow diagram, then identify loops, roadblocks, and unnecessary tasks. Then realistic subgoals were established—for example, that all order information be entered by sales within 24 hours after receipt of the order.

The team identified 12 premanufacturing steps in the original process shown in Figure 7.5, which consumed 12 days and cost $1400 to complete. Specific recommendations were to

- Eliminate Steps 1 through 5, and enter orders directly into a general order database accessible to product design, manufacturing, and other functions.

- Develop checklists from which outside and inside salespeople can verify the completeness of order information.

- Establish similar multifunctional teams to study Steps 10 through 12 to reduce their duration by two days.

As a result of these actions

- The premanufacturing process was simplified to one step, entering order into the database (originally Step 6), reducing elapsed time from 10 days to one, and cost from $1400 to $700.

Cost/Unit*
Dollars

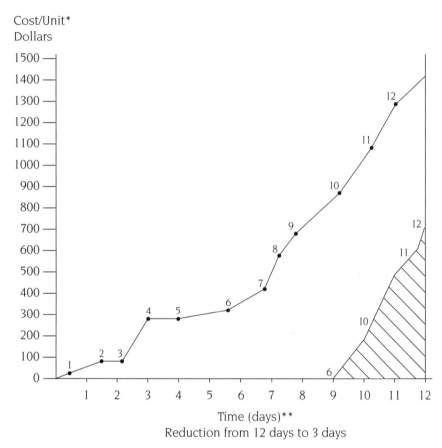

Time (days)**
Reduction from 12 days to 3 days

Ledger:
1. Log and stamp purchase order (PO)
2. Issue local file jacket
3. Recheck order for accuracy
4. Resolve discrepancies
5. Issue general order (GO) from local master file
6. Enter order into database
7. Review order "kick-outs"
8. Reenter order
9. Engineer every order
10. Schedule order into factory queue
11. Acknowledge order to field
12. Release manufacturing information (MI) and drawings

*Cost/unit is based on $30 per hour of actual time worked on the order.
**Time (days) is based on elapsed time.

Used with permission of Westinghouse Productivity and Quality Center.

Figure 7.5. The 12 steps needed before manufacturing a circuit breaker were reduced to four, cutting elapsed time from 12 days to three and cost per unit from $1400 to $700, based on $30 per hour of actual time worked on the order. Other benefits include a new attitude of cooperation and recognition of customers' needs among all employees.

- The original Steps 10 through 12 are now completed in two days. Manufacturing loads are more level throughout a given month, raising productivity and reducing costs.

- The entire process from order entry to delivery was reduced from 22 days to seven, with the realistic potential of further reductions to three, since the real time needed to complete the entire process—including manufacturing—is only three hours!

- All employees of the division are now more clearly focused on the needs of customers rather than on protecting their own turf.

The Opportunities and Benefits are Clear

There is no question that end users and internal customers expect leaps in total quality far beyond their expectations of only a few years ago. Today, product quality (whether the product is tangible or intangible) is almost a given and is the ticket for admission to most negotiations for orders. Competitive advantage and customer satisfaction are defined increasingly by the aura of information that accompanies the products. This aura of information both begins and ends with the end-user customer. Information initially is transferred by the salesperson to internal customers, who process it in various ways and for various purposes. Processed information is transferred back to the end user by the salesperson.

Regardless of direction, the information must be timely, relevant, and accurate, which means it must be compiled, processed, and communicated by employees who know, without doubt, that anything less will be detrimental to the business and their livelihoods.

The holistic approach to total quality management—holistic because it begins and ends with end-user customers and encompasses all functions of the business—can succeed only with the strong advocacy of top managers, requisite #1 put forth in *Bringing Total Quality to Sales*.[6] Their broadest spans of control and influence allow the deepest possible understanding of the domino effect of information that fails the tests of timeliness, relevancy, and accuracy.

Still another key to success is the formation and functioning of cross-functional teams to address and resolve the issues of total quality management. With a unified focus on the needs of customers, members of such teams lose their turf-protecting instincts and accompanying egocentricity, their need to be rewarded as individuals rather than as a business. Communications among members become more open and complete, allowing ideas to be put forth more freely and recommendations to be implemented quickly and effectively.

EPILOGUE

The diversity of the companies profiled in this book demonstrates conclusively that businesses of any size or type can benefit by applying total quality to sales. Diversity also demonstrates that every business is unique and that the sales process of every business is unique as well. It's this uniqueness that shapes and directs the emphases on certain aspects of total quality management as it is applied to sales.

It follows, then, that each reader's business and its sales process are unique, perhaps in ways that haven't been considered before reading this book. We encourage readers to examine their sales process and explore its uniqueness, then apply total quality management to its entirety, just as managers of our example companies have done so effectively.

The benefits can be enormous, as discussed in chapter 1 and each of the case studies.

It is the authors' fondest hope that this book will help readers reap those benefits as well.

NOTES

1. The relationships between suppliers and purchasers formed by the group transcend *contractual* to the more desirable win-win *partnerships* needed for total quality improvements for all parties.

2. The broad application of product reengineering, cloning, or reverse engineering has virtually eliminated, in many industries, the possibility of gaining competitive advantage by product differentiation. The Japanese recognized this truism many years ago when they reallocated research and development budgets from a primary focus on product design to one-third product design and two-thirds process design. The budgets of American companies tend to be just the reverse. The opinion of the authors is that the allocations of Japanese firms will prove correct over the long term, despite the present difficulties faced by Japanese industry.

3. W. Edwards Deming, *Out of the Crisis* (Cambridge, Mass.: Massachusetts Institute for Technology, 1982).

4. Many companies in the United States have freely shared their strategies for total quality management, perhaps because everyone realizes that no one organization owns a monopoly on knowledge of what works and that shared knowledge that leads to competitive advantage everywhere will lead to competitive advantage for the country and a greater share of global commerce. Westinghouse pioneered the corporate Productivity and Quality Center and was an early proponent of sharing the strategies, concepts, methods, and tools that were applied successfully at its various plants, sales offices, research and development laboratories, and other facilities.

5. The seven Baldrige criteria are as follows: Leadership, information and analysis, strategic quality planning, human resource development and management, management of process quality, quality and operational results, and customer focus and satisfaction.

6. Cas Welch and Pete Geissler, *Bringing Total Quality to Sales* (Milwaukee, Wis.: ASQC Quality Press, 1992).

INDEX